Also by David Lehman

POETRY

Yeshiva Boys (2009)
When a Woman Loves a Man (2005)
The Evening Sun (2002)
The Daily Mirror (2000)
Valentine Place (1996)
Operation Memory (1990)
An Alternative to Speech (1986)

NONFICTION

A Fine Romance: Jewish Songwriters, American Songs (2009)
The Last Avant-Garde: The Making of the New York School of Poets (1998)
The Big Question (1994)
The Line Forms Here (1992)
Signs of the Times: Deconstruction and the Fall of Paul de Man (1991)
The Perfect Murder: A Study in Detection (1989)

COLLABORATIONS

Poetry Forum (with Judith Hall) (2007)
Jim and Dave Defeat the Masked Man (with James Cummins; drawings by Archie Rand) (2006)

EDITED BY DAVID LEHMAN

The Best American Poetry (series editor)
The Best American Erotic Poems: From 1800 to the Present (2008)
The Oxford Book of American Poetry (2006)
Great American Prose Poems: From Poe to the Present (2003)
The KGB Bar Book of Poems (with Star Black) (2000)
Ecstatic Occasions, Expedient Forms (1995)
James Merrill: Essays in Criticism (with Charles Berger) (1983)
Beyond Amazement: New Essays on John Ashbery (1980)

New and Selected Poems

David Lehman

SCRIBNER POETRY

New York   London   Toronto   Sydney   New Delhi

SCRIBNER POETRY
A Division of Simon & Schuster, Inc.
1230 Avenue of the Americas
New York, NY 10020

First Scribner trade paperback edition November 2013

SCRIBNER POETRY and design are registered trademarks of The Gale Group, Inc.,
used under license by Simon & Schuster, Inc., the publisher of this work.

For information about special discounts for bulk purchases,
please contact Simon & Schuster Special Sales at 1-866-506-1949
or business@simonandschuster.com.

The Simon & Schuster Speakers Bureau can bring authors to your live event.
For more information or to book an event contact the Simon & Schuster Speakers
Bureau at 1-866-248-3049 or visit our website at www.simonspeakers.com.

DESIGNED BY ERICH HOBBING

Manufactured in the United States of America

10 9 8 7 6 5 4 3 2 1

Library of Congress Control Number: 2013031847

ISBN 978-1-4767-3187-2
ISBN 978-1-4767-3188-9 (ebook)

for Stacey

Contents

I

Escape Artist: New Poems (2013)   1

Sixteen Tons   3
On the Beautiful and Sublime   5
Reality Check   7
The Great Psychiatrist   9
Mother Died Today   10
The Laffer Curve   11
Story of My Life   12
Yours the Moon   15
The Breeders' Cup   16
Three "Dialogues of One"   18
Why I Love "You"   20
Autumn Evening   24
Talking to the Present   25
The Models   27
Sermon on the Mount   28
The Formula   29
Any Place I Hang My Hat   31
The Count   33
The Ides of March   34
The Escape Artist   35

Ghost Story   37
1977   39
Lost Weekend   42
In the Queen's Chambers   44
Zone   47
Goethe's Nightsong   53
Cento: The True Romantics   54

II

Selected Poems (1974–2009)

from *Yeshiva Boys* (2009)   55

On Purpose   57
Confessions of a Mask   58
Homily   59
The Real Thing   60
Election Day   62
Money   63
L'Shana Tova   64
Paris, 1971   67
French Movie   71
Desolation Row   73
Yeshiva Boys   74
Epilogue   89

from *When a Woman Loves a Man* (2005)   91

The Magician   93
In Freud's House   94
The Human Factor   97
Who He Was   98

Dante Lucked Out   101
Radio   102
A History of Modern Poetry   103
Like a Party   104
Wittgenstein's Ladder   105
Anna K.   109
Brooklyn Bridge   111
The Party of Ideas   115
The Prophet's Lantern   116
The Code of Napoleon   118
The Gift   121
When a Woman Loves a Man   122

from *The Evening Sun: A Journal in Poetry* (2002)   125

January 1, 8, 20, 23   127
February 11, 21, 28   129
March 8, 30   131
April 24   132
May 26   132
June 4   133
July 20   134
August 16, 25   134
September 5, 7   135
October 2, 11   137
November 14, 22   138
December 8, 30   139

from *The Daily Mirror: A Journal in Poetry* (2000)   141

January 1, 5, 14, 24, 26   143
February 6   146

March 4, 11, 15, 24, 30 146
April 2, 3, 6, 9, 15, 26, 27 or 28, 29 149
May 2, 6, 10 154
July 13, 15 156
October 11 157
November 10, 13, 17, 19, 23, 26 157
December 12, 14, 17, 29 161

from *Valentine Place* (1996) 165

Wedding Song 167
Breeze Marine 168
Boy with Red Hair 171
Flashback 174
Who She Was 175
The World Trade Center 178
Sexism 179
from "Valentine Place"
   First Lines 180
   Second Thoughts 181
   Sixth Sense 181
   Tenth Commandment 182
   Eleventh Hour 183
   Last Words 183
The Choice 185
Dark Passage 186
On the Run 187
A Little History 188
The Secret Life 191
Dutch Interior 195
The Theory of the Leisure Class 196
Stages on Life's Way 198
The End of the Affair 200

from *Operation Memory* (1990)   203

Pascal's Wager   205
Perfidia   209
One Size Fits All: A Critical Essay   210
With Tenure   212
Spontaneous Combustion   214
The Survivors   215
The Answering Stranger   218
Rejection Slip   221
The Desire for Strange Cities   222
Mythologies   224
Operation Memory   244
Fear   246
New York City, 1974   247
Cambridge, 1972   252
For I Will Consider Your Dog Molly   256

from *An Alternative to Speech* (1986)   259

Enigma Variations   261
Glose   264
The Master of Ceremonies   266
Gift Means Poison in German   268
Shake the Superflux!   270
Ode   272
The Thirty-nine Steps   274
The Difference Between Pepsi and Coke   276
Sonnet   277
The More You Have to Lose   278

III

Early and Uncollected Poems   279

Literal Lives (1989)   281
Nirvana (1978)   282
October Classic (1973)   284
Robert Desnos (1973)   285
Simplicity (1972)   286
from "Goodbye Instructions" (1970–1972)   287
Traces (1967)   291
The Presidential Years (1967)   292

Notes   299

Acknowledgments   303

Note

W. H. Auden, in the foreword to his *Collected Shorter Poems, 1927–1957*, writes that he "sometimes shuffled poems so as to bring together those related by theme or genre" but "in the main their order is chronological." I have allowed myself the same liberty while organizing the contents of this book in reverse chronological order by date of composition. (The daily poems from *The Evening Sun* and *The Daily Mirror*, assembled according to the calendar, provide a kind of backspin.) The earliest poems here date to 1967; the most recent, forty-five years later. Some poems were written long before they were collected in a volume of my poetry. "For I Will Consider Your Dog Molly" and "When a Woman Loves a Man" are two examples of poems written nearly ten years before they appeared in a book. In several cases where the work was set aside, revised, and completed (or abandoned), sometimes years after its inception, I let instinct dictate where in the contents I should place the poem. —DL

I

Escape Artist:

New Poems (2013)

Sixteen Tons

To prolong the moment
as a simile extends a sentence
about the heroine's innocence
which she yielded to her lover and now
she hates him as Eve hates Adam
when she risks her life
to give birth to their child—

To sit in your car and listen
to the last bars of something great
(Bernstein's "Divertimento for Orchestra,"
you find out later) and then you turn off
the engine, open the door
and return to your life, "another
day older and deeper in debt"—

That's what the authorities fail to get.

You can learn a lot from
the sportscaster's present tense:
"Three years ago he beats out that hit,"
about a player who has lost a step or two
due to a leg injury.
Three years ago, we all beat out that hit.

When I escape from this party
of unloved doves and loveless hawks,

I shall head to my desk and write
the sonnet that praises the antique pen
used to write out prophecies of today
with you on my arm, unafraid.

On the Beautiful and Sublime

> Knowledge is beautiful; understanding is sublime.
> —Kant

1.

Radio is a hot medium;
Television, a cool one.

A train ride in Russia is a novel.
A train ride to Chicago is a movie.
A flight to Miami is a disaster movie.

A yew tree is a poem.
A banyan tree is the prose
Of Ralph Waldo Emerson.

A woman's undergarments (any epoch) are poetry.
A man's undergarments (any epoch) are prose.

Panties (white, silk, high-rise) are beautiful.
Jockstraps are sublime.

Paranoia is poetry.
Insomnia is prose.

2.

Death by lethal injection is prose.
Death by hanging is infernal.
Death by firing squad is the noble sublime.

Homer is the tragic sublime.
Cigarettes are sublime.

Cigars are sublime.
Pipes are beautiful.

The Song of Songs is beautiful,
Genesis and Job are sublime.

Isaiah is sublime. Samuel I and II are sublime.
Ruth is beautiful and sublime.
Wordsworth is sublime. Keats is sublime and beautiful.

Knowledge is beautiful,
Understanding is sublime.

Reality Check

1.

In the last analysis—does anyone still use that phrase?
it's a great fake phrase, like "the moment of truth"
which Nabokov ridiculed so convincingly—
you can be sure of two things.
One is that Congress is going to kick the can down the road.
You know it, I know it, but somebody who doesn't know it
can turn a sucker bet into a sucker punch and that is the essence
of what we call a derivative. And today we like to bank on the VIX,
which measures volatility as the square root of variance.

2.

My friend Ajax (who used to play hockey for the Islanders)
says he is a momentum investor, leery of value traps,
and didn't recognize my wife because he has "facial blindness."
He looked me in the eye like a marshal in a Western
and said, "What was the other thing
that we can be sure of?" I sold him on derivatives.
It seemed an act of kindness to lie.

"It could be a game changer," I said, knowing the phrase
would get him to take out his checkbook.

"We've passed the point of no return,"

he said as we shook hands.
"We always do," I said.
"What about the long run?" he asked,
lighting a cigar with the fifty-dollar bill
he had used to snort white powder
from a mirror to his nostrils.
"In the long run," I said, "we are all dead."
"Keynes," he said, recognizing the quote.
"Canes," I said, helping him to the door.

The Great Psychiatrist

I visited him three times. The first visit we spoke about T. S. Eliot's play *The Cocktail Party* and the character he reminded me of, a sort of spiritual psychiatrist: a no-nonsense male authority figure with T. S. Eliot's world-weary deep rueful skeptical intellect, the waspish sting neutralized by Anglican gentleness with a smile of resignation. It was a scary but fascinating ordeal—talking to him, I mean. The fact that his first name was Eliot may have had something to do with it. I went home and reread the play and I saw it performed on Broadway and in London's West End. When I talked to him about it, I realized that one out of every ten of Eliot's analysands is a martyr in the making, preparing to make the ultimate sacrifice in a South American revolution or a famine in Africa. "One out of ten," Eliot agreed. "But not you and not me." The third time I visited him we played a game of free association. He would say "death wish" and I would say "pleasure principle" and then we reversed roles, and I would say "pleasure principle" and he would say "death wish." The sessions had a profound effect on me. It was after the last visit that I understood that these two impulses, the death wish and the pleasure principle, meet at the point of orgasm. From this insight everything else followed: job, wife, children.

Mother Died Today

Mother died today. That's how it began. Or maybe yesterday, I can't be sure. I gave the book to my mother in the hospital. She read the first sentence. Mother died today. She laughed and said you sure know how to cheer me up. The telegram came. It said, Mother dead Stop Funeral tomorrow Stop. Mother read it in the hospital and laughed at her college boy son. Or maybe yesterday, I don't remember. Mama died yesterday. The telegram arrived a day too late. I had already left. Europe is going down, the euro is finished, and what does it matter? My mother served plum cake and I read the page aloud. Mother died today or yesterday and I can't be sure and it doesn't matter. Germany can lose two world wars and still rule all of Europe, and does it matter whether you die at thirty or seventy? Mother died today. It was Mother's Day, the day she died, the year she died. In 1940 it was the day the Germans marched into Belgium and France and Churchill succeeded Chamberlain as Prime Minister. The telegram came from the asylum, the home, the hospital, the "assisted living" facility, the hospice, the clinic. Your mother passed away. Heartfelt condolences. The price of rice is going up, and what does it matter? I'll tell you what I told the nurse and anyone that asks. Mother died today.

(May 10, 2012)

The Laffer Curve

On the back of a restaurant napkin he composed
the definitive exposition of the theory
that the economy is driven or decisively
restrained by the federal income tax rate,
and a lot of people went along with that, because
it was in their interest to do so but also because
he made the argument so casually and lent his apt name
to the diagram describing a direct ratio
between tax rates and the rate of unemployment.

That was an economist named Laffer, Arthur Laffer.

But I heard the news on the radio and in my mind
there was a curve that a mathematician had devised
to measure the success or failure of a comic endeavor
with highest honors awarded to practical jokes
that turn out to have a major influence on history
despite their intent to be just funny, a harmless
diversion, demonstrating that the last laugh,
whether bitter or hollow or even downright mirthless,
is always at the expense of the losers.

Story of My Life

There must be dozens of poems with the title "Story of My Life."
Maybe even hundreds.
It's a natural, a meme—which is pronounced to rhyme with team, by
      the way,
though I keep thinking it should be *même*, as in the French word for
      "same."
It is spelled m-e-m-e and examples include self-replicating phrases,
"knock knock" jokes, an almost *au courant* idiom like "same old same
      old,"
or a beer jingle, Émile Waldteufel's "Estudiantina" waltz (op. 191)
      adapted to the needs
of a Brooklyn-based brewery named after a Wagner opera, Rheingold.
"My beer is Rheingold the dry beer. Think of Rheingold whenever you
      buy beer.
It's not bitter, not sweet, it's the extra dry treat,
Won't you try extra dry Rheingold beer?"
What memories that jingle stirs up, mostly about the futility
of the New York Mets, whose on-the-air sponsor was Rheingold beer.

Anyway, this meme, "story of my life," has the virtues all clichés have:
You can rejuvenate it, jolt some meaning back into it, while honoring
      the vernacular,
and to do that is a challenge for young poets, and an opportunity,
and so every year a poet on the faculty somewhere is asking his or her
      students
to write the poem in them that finds its inspiration in the title "Story
      of My Life."

It's not a form exactly but a prompt, an assignment, an idea for a poem,
like getting everybody to pick photographs of themselves as teenagers
and write poems triggered by the associations.
The assumption is that everybody has a story to tell,
a sad story perhaps but one full of hidden corners and exciting detours,
and the trick is to tell the story as succinctly as possible,
it being understood that by "story" the poet means
not a narrative so much as the suggestion of one, an enigmatic anecdote
the length of a Zen koan or a poem by Stephen Crane,
that can serve as the allegory of the writer's life.

And today, as I sit here in the yard of 105 Valentine Place in Ithaca
hoping to get some sun
at this time of day when the angle of vision is perfect
and I can survey my properties:
the passing clouds that mask the yellow sheen
of old man sun, and the gray clouds that are drifting off like his daughters,
and here comes the blue, patches of it, and clouds like big balls of cotton,
the new hemlock, the adolescent juniper, the old reliable quince bush,
and three dark, tall, and graceful pines that stand sentry over the pre-
        sunset celebrations
of evening, another job accomplished, another day in the book—

I sit here, just as I wanted to do all day,
with my legs and arms warmed by the sun,
with my notebook and my pen in hand,
and I am the Daddy of all the scene,
knowing the sun and the clouds, the wind pushing them
and even the stately evergreen with clusters of yellow nuts on its branches
are performing for my benefit and at my command—

I sit here, as I wanted to do, and the breeze grazes my cheeks
and there are bowls of plums and white-flesh peaches
and a sweet-smelling melon on the table beside me,
and the day offers other enticements to come:
a swim in a blue pool followed by dinner prepared by Stacey
for me and special guest son Joe,
grilled swordfish steaks with the pesto sauce Stacey concocted,

a salad of heirloom and beefsteak tomatoes, pasta punctuated with corn,
and a bottle of premium sparkling Blanc de Blancs.

And so, now that I have it, what do I do with the happiness of this
        moment?
I, who never took a writing workshop but have taught many,
think of how I would handle the assignment for next week's class.
I write about a boy, not me but like me, in green tennis shirt
and khaki shorts, a blue baseball cap and well-worn brown moccasins,
and the boy wants nothing more than to sit in the sun
but always arrives too late: the diagonal line dividing the yard
into equal areas of sun and shade
vanishes as soon as he gets there.
That's all. I write it in the third person, call it "Story of My Life."

Yours the Moon

Yours the moon
mine the Milky
Way a scarf

around my neck
I love you
as the night

loves the moon's
dark side as
the sky, distant,

endless, wears her
necklace of stars
over her dress

under my scarf
that she wears
against the cold

The Breeders' Cup

1. To the Fates

They cannot keep the peace
or their hands off each other,
breed not, yet preach
the old discredited creed.

Love is charity conceived
as a coin dropped
in a beggar's cup.
Reason not the need.

Gluttony is no nicer than greed
or wrath, but lust
is our categorical must.
We have no choice but to breed.

2. Olympia

Olympia lies on her couch
with an insolent stare,
her hand hiding her crotch,
a flower in her hair.

She splits the lot of us with a sneer:
We are either breeders or queer.

We will fight wars because of her.
She will root us on. We will win.

The face in the mirror is not brave,
but we crave contact with her skin
and the jewel in the mouth of her cave.
She tempts like a sin

and we fall
into a deep enchanted sleep,
and wake up ready to make the leap,
ready to heed her call,

only now we're alone,
a platoon of ex-pals in Manhattan,
on streets less friendly than wilderness.
She tempts like a sin

but then sends us home to the wife,
commands us to resume the life
we had planned to give up in her honor:
the life of a dutiful husband, a modest success

in his profession, impressive
in credentials, in mood depressive
(but nothing that a pill won't cure).
You ask if he is happy? "Sure."

And Olympia lies on her couch,
with her insolent stare,
her hand hiding her crotch,
a flower in her hair.

Three "Dialogues of One"

"What you call freedom
I call privilege
what you call law
I call biology
what you call liberty
I call pornography"

"What you call necessity
I call capital
what you call poverty
I call subsidy
what you call pornography
I call art
what you call crime
I call freedom"

*

"Say Pop
how come
you talk
about 'this
country' as
if you
from another
country come?"

"But I
do from
another
country
come"

*

"The beauty of your skin
is my sin," said Adam to Eve
in the garden.

(The face in the mirror
swims to the surface
and sees her face there.)

"When we lie together
for warmth in winter,
the beauty of our sin

produces our kin,"
said Eve to Adam
in the garden.

Why I Love "You"

for Stacey

A woman in California asked me whether I have a favorite word and if so what is it? I said my favorite word is "you." I love "you." She was disappointed. I think she expected me to opt for "mellifluous" or "sibilance" or some other onomatopoeic special.

But pronouns in a poem or prose poem function as unknowns do in algebra, and "you" is the most versatile one out there. The word means the same singular and plural, and it is gender-free, so it can conceal not only identity but sex and number. This makes "you" as useful as "it" and even more complicated from the epistemological point of view. "You" can be Albert or Albertine, and no one need be the wiser.

When I say "you" in a poem, I immediately establish a certain intimacy even if the words "I" and "you" in the specific case are pronominal fictions representing abstract entities, imaginary selves, characters in a dream, the author and the reader. Thus T. S. Eliot begins his love song: "Let us go then, you and I, / When the evening is spread out against the sky." Join me in this adventure. Mr. J. Alfred Prufrock may lack confidence. But I, the author, am as suave a seducer as you are likely to meet.

Many claustrophobic poems would get an instant oxygen infusion if you were to add a second person, you, to the I-dominated mix. In "I Believe in You," one of the great songs in Frank Loesser's *How to Succeed in Business Without Really Trying*, Robert Morse sings to himself, to his mirror image in the executive washroom, while the man's rivals harmonize ("gotta stop that man") and their electric razors provide the kazoo-like percussion. Yet this hymn to an egocentric hero can, stripped from its theatrical context, serve quite well as a lady's declaration of love to her dreamboat.

You and I form a joint conspiracy. In Robert Frost's "Meeting and Passing," a man and a woman who are destined to become lovers meet by chance on a path. After exchanging greetings, they resume walking in their opposite directions. This is how the poem ends: "Afterward I went past what you had passed / Before we met and you what I had passed." The last line is a small wonder, not least because of its compression and because its iambs fall emphatically on the two verbs, the pronouns "you" and "I," and the second half of "Before." The moment "we met," over too soon, was the moment poised between "before" and "after" as each of us enters the other's past, which is also his or her own future.

In grammar the first and second persons combine to form the first person plural: I plus you equal we. And we also equal something else. When we go to bed, "we two being one, are it," John Donne writes in "The Canonization" about the consummation of love, the momentary unity of the sexes combined into a higher entity. But these pronouns are slippery. Can we identify "I" with the ego, "it" with the id, "we" with the superego, and "you" with the other, imagined or real, a substitute for the parent of the opposite sex, exerting a force beyond the pleasure principle? Not necessarily, although it's tempting to twist this Freudian conceit into a full-blown story, where "you" equals death, a beautiful blonde angel with a slight lisp, who sings her seductive song while Odysseus is lashed to the mast.

Ask yourself the question the surrealists struggled over: "Death—male or female?" Then consider the same question only with "you" instead of "death."

In her villanelle "One Art," Elizabeth Bishop lists, in ascending order of significance, the losses that she has futilely tried to master over the course of a lifetime. First to go are "lost door keys, the hour badly spent." Then, in a sentence where "you" means *one* or maybe *I*, comes the loss of "places, and names, and where it was you meant / to travel." In the fourth stanza, "my mother's watch" and "three loved houses went." The fifth and penultimate stanza widens the focus: the speaker mourns "some realms I owned, two rivers, a continent." But the final stanza trumps all with the mention of "losing you."

Without "you" I would be as lonesome as Adam in Eden lacking free will. I need "you" as life needs to end in death. Without you there would be no sin, no sex, no history, no temptation, no chance for immortality. Are these rationalizations? Maybe, but that's better than the endless quarreling between Adam and Eve that follows the eating of the forbidden fruit in the ninth book of *Paradise Lost*. The pungency of "fruitless" and the double meaning of "vain" in Milton's lines make the point: "Thus they in mutual accusation spent / The fruitless hours, but neither self-condemning; / And of their vain contest appear'd no end."

Whatever else they are, "I" and "you" represent the first dichotomy. "I" is to *either* as "you" is to *or*—the second person always introduces the possibility of disagreement, if not dissent. An ordinary fork in the road acquires an additional level of complexity if it is approached by two rather than one. Or maybe "I" and "you" are two lines that intersect, as the rue de Rennes and the boulevard Raspail meet in Paris, before going their separate ways. And in an early chapter, the novel's hero and heroine, still unknown to each other, will cross the street in opposite directions or ride the same number 11 bus in London between the statue of Wellington on Threadneedle Street and the Albert pub on Victoria Street with its Irish flags in the window, it being St. Patrick's Day.

"A man and a woman are one," Wallace Stevens observes, though the metamorphoses don't end there. Others enter the picture. "A man and a woman and a blackbird are one."

When Andrew Marvell writes, "Two paradises 'twere in one / To live in paradise alone," his mathematical metaphor is crucial to his defense of solitude. Just as "alone" contains "one," I without you am one individual, unified, undivided, living in two paradises. One is the absence of time. The other is the absence of "you."

Yet who can resist the lure of the second person? Without her, with whom would I quarrel or link? She brings the fruit of knowledge to me and I eat, and we have invented free will, which is synonymous with rebellion. Free will, free fall. Yet we feel tall. We are the gods of Romanticism, you and I, swaggering like Antony willing to kiss away his kingdom for a mirth.

The difference between "I love you still" and "I love you again" is the subject of tomorrow's debate.

In brief, "you" mean more than the world to me.

Autumn Evening

after Hölderlin

The yellow pears hang in the lake.
Life sinks, grace reigns, sins ripen, and
in the north dies an almond tree.

A genius took me by the hand and said
come with me though the time has not yet come.

Therefore, when the gods get lonely,
a hero will emerge from the bushes
of a summer evening
bearing the first green figs of the season.

For the glory of the gods has lain asleep
too long in the dark
in darkness too long
too long in the dark.

Talking to the Present

O beloved present
tense you let
us lead late
breaking lives so
we do we
go out we
go in we're
on the go
all the time
thanks to you.

O I know
there are days
when nothing less
than the past,
over and done
with, will do:
"She left," not
"she was leaving."
He saw her
leave. He kept
seeing her leave.

So days go
and so too
tomorrow comes too
soon for some

not fast enough
for others and
yet we still
can't sit still
love the rain
embrace the light
and talk to
the present begging
it to stay.

The Models

She be the secretary, he be the boss.
She be the blonde, he be the man.

She be the skirt, he be the pants.
She wear the panties, he smoke the blunt.

She wear the makeup, he wear her scent.
She wear the man, he cover the lover.

He be business, she be nervous.
He take her to kiki, she write kiki.

She write kiki and phone number.
He bow to her as she leave the bus.

She be the hunter, he be the prey.
He be the car, she be the highway.

She be the site of his construction.
He be the height of her insurrection.

Sermon on the Mount

Ye spirits that hover above,
bear witness to my quest
and I shall prove
as tall a teller of tales
as ever stopped a wedding guest.

If love sometimes fails,
does lust never lie?
The truth is acted out in bed.
On manna and honeydew fed,
the dreamers moan and sigh.

Can you divorce the act
of love from the fact
of death? When her lover
left her, she went undercover
yet kept her illusions intact.

Bitter constraint, in darkness bred,
carves a living monument of lust,
a nymph obedient, with upraised head,
kneeling before him in whom she trusts,
in the chapel where her hormones led.

The Formula

"Some people would pay a lot of money for that information."
It wasn't said with menace, but that was the effect.
In her purse she had the tiniest camera
anyone in the control room had ever seen.
Like many widows her age she had transferred
her suspicion from the Germans to the Russians.
Berlin remained the center of the struggle,
which it had been since 1945 and maybe even earlier.
Of little use to her now was the pistol she kept in her underwear drawer.
Love had left her life except in its abstract and spiritual forms,
yet in her loins desire waxed and waned with the moon.
She had a matter-of-fact attitude toward sex.
It had been months since her last confession.

The formula was encrypted in a postcard of the Stephansdom
she had given her niece to mail to London
from the postbox at Friedmanngasse 52
three weeks and four cities ago, but
the man in the black trench coat couldn't know that.
"I shall have to ask you to come with me,"
he said, and she tried to place the accent.
Latvia? The Ukraine? They were arguing about something
inside, but the voices subsided when they led her into the room.
"Relax. If I wanted you dead, you'd have been—"
He left the sentence unfinished. "Oh yes," he said,
"I've had my eyes on you. Your perfume is nice,
very nice, but you may not get to wear it

where you're going." At his signal the others left the room.
"Unless—" There was a bottle of whiskey
and two shot glasses. Outside the fog rolled in
and dour men in motor caps rowed their small craft
in the canal to the base of the dungeon
while two black cars idled down the road.

Any Place I Hang My Hat

In Amsterdam or Copenhagen,
Or any harbor that is a haven,
I did as I was told:
I wrote god it came out gold.
Many stole. I got caught.
I was the lucky thirteenth caller
Who heard the verdict in time's cellar.
They said I would be shot.

In this place or that,
Or any place I hang my hat,
They never called me sir.
But god did I love fighting with her
In college in New Haven
Where minds were bought
And minds were sold
For ten cents on the dollar.

I heard the verdict in time's cellar.
She was the buyer. I was the seller.
When we opened in New Haven,
She quipped it was no heaven.
But god did I love fighting with her,
Before and after writhing with her,
In this place or that
Or any place I hang my hat.

If wishes and deeds were one,
And nothing new under the sun,
Absent us not from felicity awhile;
Rather behold the face of heaven
Contort into the shape of a smile
As we stroll down the aisle
In Amsterdam or Copenhagen
Or any harbor that is a haven.

The Count

The count on the hitter in a baseball game is as close as you get to the draw in poker. The difference between a one-ball, one-strike count and a two-ball, one-strike count is, from the hitter's point of view, like the difference between two queens with one showing when three cards have been dealt and two queens with one showing when four cards have been dealt. The player must calculate the odds, and do it quickly, on an absolute basis and in relation to the hands of the other players. This operation of the rational intellect must be combined with the gambler's educated intuition, and all the while a deadpan must be maintained. Finally the player bets. I say finally because it seems as if much has happened, yet in reality only seconds have gone by. It is similar for the batter in a baseball game, who must calculate the odds of seeing a fastball, a curve ball, or a change-up, as well as its intended location, as the count goes from two balls and one strike to two balls and two strikes—or to the much more favorable count of three balls and one strike. The batter steps out of the box. Maybe he has some special ritual, like kicking up a little dirt with his right spike. He gets back into the box. The pitch comes, he guesses fastball, high, and here it is, big as a melon. He's going to bet all he has on this swing. He's all in.

The Ides of March

The origin of every fortune is a crime.
The ides of March are a dangerous time.

The ideas of March originate in wind.
Madness may spring from a mind that hasn't sinned.

The guides of March have scary stories to tell.
The family money came from a corpse and an oil well.

The editors of March fly to the moon and bring back April.
The original sinner has learned to shave and say "I will."

You can trace each legacy back to the day
when the id of March exposed the ego's feet of clay.

The dice of March roll on the green felt tabletop.
The suicides of March drive past the octagonal sign: Stop!

On the dais of March sit the deceased father and mother.
Every happy family is different from every other.

The Escape Artist

A dark green room: the experiment fails,
And the leaves change color before their time.
He felt, though he had not committed a crime,
Like a gangster disguised in a top hat and tails,

Entering the lady's East Village apartment
To seduce her. If he should arrive out of breath,
It's because he knows he has a date with death,
Though that's not what the church fathers meant.

She called him a romantic fool, but she didn't mean
To make him feel bad. She just wanted to love him
In the attic, where the lights had grown dim.
Yet the darkness was green, however drab the scene,

Where danger took him by the hand, and the heroine
In his arms was someone he had met before,
In a novel about a murderer and a whore,
And didn't expect to meet again

In the seedy familiar hotel room with the bullets flying
All around them. They were busy dying,
But the imaginary spies of childhood were still spying
On them, the sinful and tormented ones,

Hungry for ordinary corrupt human love, and bound
To turn up wherever a lively crisis could be found:
A lost breed, the sort of chap who knew all about guns,
Having used them for Russian roulette, and won.

Ghost Story

1.

You could see it in their faces:
the foreknowledge of their own absence,
rare in anyone but almost unknown in a child.

Unlike us they sensed it from the start. They knew
that people, when they die, stay where they are,
only now they're as invisible as a star
in daylight, forbidden to act but free to comment,
for no one will hear them now, except us, who
in our weaker moments think of ourselves
as ghosts, the casualties of calamities
that happened before we were born.

2.

All this was clear now, a couple of decades after
the fact, and the job had fringe benefits, too,
though the people in personnel couldn't tell you what
they were: only you knew the secret, and you had sworn
to keep it to yourself. None of them suspected it,
not even the shyster who agreed to take your case,
to whom you tried to explain the paradox of freedom:

Like a wish granted by a capricious genie, it is
predicated on the condition that you never use it,
never exercise it in defiance of the authorities.
And that is why you see us here, like Marius
contemplating the ruins of Carthage,
among the monuments that incite the poor to vandalism
though like us they're invisible to the naked eye.

And the children who believed in us are gone.

1977

We used to live nearer to the sky
and seldom got dizzy looking down
from the tops of the trees
on blue summer eves. Europe called us.

We went. At the time we were
a large Russian émigré family
destined to replicate the same living room
in Paris, Geneva, Milan, and Berlin.

The cypresses in the south of France looked
like fingers—like dead men's fingers.
Every cemetery had them. One puff
at La Victoire and he was smoking again.

Climb these colonnades, this spiral staircase,
and hear history in the making. Join the masses
below listening to speeches from balconies
hanging on every word. "And if

the concentration camps were predicted
by Dante and the devout, that changes nothing."
The Americans were so damn naïve.
You guys think you can come in,

wave some dollars, make a lot of noise,
watch a burlesque show in Montmartre,

make more noise, and we're supposed to have
peace in Europe, the socialist scoffed.

The dictator folded his arms.
The women practiced the walking habits of cats.
They displayed their legs to him alone,
who separated their latent meaning from their manifest content.

The waiter with the circumflex mustache hovered.
The addition was wrong, but he was imperturbable.
He was in love. Never had he seen
a woman lovelier than this city of bridges

and the tower standing guard over them.
Pinball machines responded to his deft handling.
He stood drinks for the house, oysters for the gang.
He organized a novel like a crossword puzzle:

the first part across, the second part down,
with clues for chapter headings.
Then came the new orders, canceling his leave.
He had to go to bleak Besançon,

where sinister hoteliers read *L'Aurore*,
eavesdropped on him, and searched his room
when he went out. Mostly he walked.
The passport changed hands in the movie

theater. A porn classic with Nazis
and blonde blue-eyed prostitutes
was playing. Twilight scattered
the pigeons in the public square.

And nothing tasted better
on such a day than a *citron pressé*,
the perfect still life (lemon, knife,
flask of water, sugar, glass, spoon)

you could drink. You don't think youth
is everlasting. You think life is tragic,
and for some it is: bright boys who die
in cars, girl prodigies dead of a rare disease.

And you were young, and survival is not
a moral achievement.
You're never as good as you're lucky
on Wall Street or at Verdun.

In retrospect, it was as if the European past
consisted of moments just like this one—
the scattering pigeons in the public square,
the afternoon in bed with a bottle of cold white wine.

The past was a succession of non sequiturs
in a deaf man's ear before history resumed
where the Europeans dreamed of going:
Los Angeles, Miami, and New York.

Lost Weekend

1. Her Movie

She was the American woman in the novel he was reading
On the train. She proved that the picture could come to life.
She didn't touch her Scotch. She fell asleep at the movies.
She told him that his photograph of her mind saved her life.

When she looked at the faces on the platforms that they passed,
They became characters in the novel she was writing.
She could tell at a glance what they did for a living,
Whom they voted for, what cars they drove, how many kids

And what they did in the dark. Whoever she was, he loved her.
He could see that now. She rubbed her eyes.
She had come in fourth in the steeplechase,

Had won no prize. Did she recognize the place?
She was prepared to impersonate his wife
Even if that meant she would have to marry him.

2. Their Finest Hour

You could read it in her eyes.
She was the mistress who said
Her husband's name in bed
With a stranger. All lies,

His promises and her vows,
But they didn't want to remember,
And they had fun playing house
Until war broke out in September.

When the firm sent him abroad, he went
To meet his fate on the Continent,
Leaving her in nurse's uniform
To care for the wounded and infirm.

This one she called "Buster," that one "Hon."
In her dream he was everyone.

3. His Memory

The knowledge that he doesn't exist—
The most liberating thought a man can have
After making love to his wife. He rubbed his eyes.
The pills had stopped working, and he was pissed,

And there were other reasons to pull down the shade.
On the pond in the park where they used to walk,
The skater kept her head pulled back
And her arms to her side, spinning without fear

Of the force that would alter her angular momentum,
Causing a certain amount of friction, and loss of heat.
He thought he could see her, but then she was gone.

In his memory he could see through her clothes, through her skin,
And a clock was ticking where her heart should have been,
And it was always ten before two or ten after ten.

In the Queen's Chambers

after Henri Michaux

When Plume arrived at the palace, credentials in hand, the Queen said to him:

"Well, then. The King is extremely busy at the moment. You may see him later. We'll go together to see him, if you'd like. Around five o'clock. That's settled then. His Majesty likes Danish people, His Majesty will be glad to receive you, perhaps while waiting you'll take a stroll with me.

"As the palace is so very large, I am always afraid of losing my way and finding myself in the kitchen, which, you understand, would be quite ridiculous for a Queen. Shall we go this way? This is one passage I'm familiar with. Here is my bedroom."

And they enter the bedroom.

"As we have two good hours ahead of us, you might perhaps read a little to me, though I don't think you'll find much of interest on my shelves. Perhaps you play cards? But I can tell you now I would lose right away. Anyway, don't your feet need a rest? Standing up is so tiring, isn't it? And sitting down isn't much of an improvement. Perhaps one can stretch out here on the sofa."

But she gets up again a moment later.

"Unbearable heat reigns in this room. If you would kindly help me undress, it would give me great pleasure. Afterwards we can have a proper talk. I would like very much to know more about Denmark. This dress slips off so easily I wonder how I managed to keep it on all day. It slips off without my even noticing. When I raise my arms, watch, even a child could do it. Of course, I wouldn't let him. I'm fond of children, but there's always such a babble in the palace, and then they do get on one's nerves."

So Plume undresses her.

"But listen, you can't stay like that. To remain fully dressed in the bedroom is exceedingly gauche, and I can't see you like that, it's as if you were about to run out and leave me all alone in this enormous palace."

And Plume gets undressed. He gets into bed wearing nothing but his shirt.

"It's still only 3:15," she says. "Do you really know so much about Denmark that you could regale me about it for the next hour and three quarters? I won't be so demanding—I understand how difficult a task it would be. Why don't I give you a bit more time to think. And look, while we're waiting, since you're already here I'll show you something I find most intriguing. I would be curious to know what a Dane will think of this.

"I have, you see, here under my right breast, three little marks. Well, actually, two little ones and a big one. See? The big one looks almost . . . it's really quite odd, isn't it, while on the left breast, nothing! All white!

"Okay, talk to me, but examine it carefully first, go slow . . ."

And Plume makes his examination. He touches, he probes with uncertain fingers, he searches for truths that will make him tremble, his fingers going round and round in their curved trajectory.

And Plume is lost in thought.

"You're wondering," the Queen says a few moments later, "(and I see now that you're an old hand at this sort of thing), you want to know if I have others. No," she says, and turns beet red.

"Now tell me about Denmark, but first lie here beside me so I can give you my full attention."

Plume approaches; he lies down beside her and now he can't conceal a thing.

And as a result:

"Listen," she says, "I thought you'd have more respect for the Queen, but, well, since you're here, I wouldn't let *that* stand in the way of our pursuit of warm relations between my country and yours."

And the Queen draws him to her.

"Caress my legs," she says, "or I'm likely to get distracted, and I won't remember why I lay down in the first place . . ."

It was at this moment that the King walked in!

. . . .

Terrible adventures, in whatever way begun and with whatever consequences, painful adventures, adventures arranged by an implacable foe.

Zone

after Guillaume Apollinaire

In the end you've had enough of the ancient world

O Eiffel Tower shepherdess today your bridges are a bleating flock

You've had it up to here with the Romans and Greeks

Here even the automobiles look like antiques
Only religion remains new religion
Retains the simplicity of an airport hanger

Alone in Europe you are not antiquated O Christianity
The most modern man in Europe is you Pope Pius X
While you whom the windows watch are too ashamed
To enter a church and confess your sins today
You read handouts pamphlets posters sing to you from up high
There's your morning poetry and for prose there are the newspapers
Paperback police thrillers for twenty-five centimes
Portraits of the great a thousand and one titles

This morning I saw a pretty little street whose name I forget
Clean and new it seemed the clarion of the sun
Executives workers and beautiful stenographers
Pass this way four times a day from Monday morning to Saturday night
Three times each morning a siren whines
An angry bell at noon

Billboards signs and murals
Shriek like parakeets
I love the grace of this industrial street
In Paris between the rue Aumont-Thiéville and the avenue des Ternes

Look how young the street is and you still only a toddler
Your mother dresses you in blue and white
You are very religious you and your old pal René Dalize
You love nothing more than church ceremonies
It's nine o'clock the gas turns blue you sneak out of the dormitory
You stay up all night praying in the school chapel
Under a globed amethyst worthy of adoration
The halo around the head of Christ revolves forever
He is the lovely lily that we cultivate
The red-haired torch immune to any wind
The pale and scarlet son of the mother of many sorrows
The evergreen tree ever hung with prayers
The twin gallows of honor and eternity
The six-pointed star
God who dies on Friday and revives on Sunday
Christ who climbs heavens higher than any aviator can reach
He holds the world's aviation record

Christ pupil of my eye
Pupil of twenty centuries he knows what he's doing
And changed into a bird this century like Jesus soars in the air
Devils in abysses lift their heads to stare
Look they say he takes after Simon Magus of Judea
They say he can steal but can also steal away
The angels vault past the all-time greatest pole vaulters
Icarus Enoch Elijah Apollonius of Tyana
Gather around the first airplane
Or make way for the elevation of those who took communion
The priests rise eternally as they raise the host
And the airplane touches down at last its wings outstretched
From heaven come flying millions of swallows
Ibises flamingoes storks from Africa
The fabled Roc celebrated by storytellers and poets

With Adam's skull in its claws the original skull
Messenger from the horizon the eagle swoops and screams
And from America the little hummingbird
From China the long and supple *pihis*
Who have one wing each and fly in pairs
Here comes the dove immaculate spirit
Escorted by lyre-bird and vain peacock
And the phoenix engendering himself from the flames
Veils everything for a moment with his sparkling cinders
The sirens leave the perilous seas
And sing beautifully when they get here all three of them
And all of them eagle phoenix and *pihi* of China
Befriend our flying machine

Now you are walking in Paris all alone among the crowds
Herds of bellowing buses roll by you
Love's anguish grips you by the throat
As if you were fated never again to be loved
In the bad old days you would have entered a monastery
You feel ashamed when you slip and catch yourself saying prayers
You mock yourself your laughter crackles like hellfire
The sparks flash in the depths of your life
Which is a painting hung in a gloomy museum
And sometimes you've got to get as close to it as you can

Today as you walk around Paris and her bloodstained women
It was (and I would just as soon not remember it was) the demise of
    beauty

Surrounded by flames our Lady looked down on me at Chartres
The blood of thy sacred heart drowned me in Montmartre
I am sick of hearing the blessed words
The love I suffer from is a shameful disease
And my image of you survives in my anguish and insomnia
It's always near you and then it fades away

Now you're at the Mediterranean shore
Under the lemon groves in flower all year long

You go sailing with your friends
One is from Nice one from Menton two Turbiasques
The creatures of the deep terrify us
The fish swimming through seaweed is the symbol of our Savior

You're in the garden of a tavern on the outskirts of Prague
You're in heaven a rose is on the table
Which you look at instead of writing your poems or your prose
You look at the bug asleep in the heart of the rose

You recognize yourself in the mosaics of St. Vitus
You almost died of grief that day
You were Lazarus crazed by daylight
In the Jewish quarter the hands on the clocks go backward
And you creep forward through the story of your life
Climbing to the Hradchin in the evening and listening
To the Czech songs in the cafés

Here you are in Marseilles amid the watermelons

Here at Koblenz at the Hotel of the Giant

Here in Rome sitting under a Japanese medlar tree

Here you are in Amsterdam with a woman who you think is beautiful
        but is really ugly
She will wed a student from Leyden
You can rent rooms by the hour *Cubicula locanda*
I remember the three days I spent there and the three at Gouda

You are in Paris summoned before a judge
Arrested like a common criminal

You journeyed in joy and despair
Before you encountered lies and old age
Love made you suffer at twenty at thirty
I've lived like a fool and wasted my time

You no longer dare to look at your hands and now I feel like crying
Over you over the one I love over everything that has scared you

Eyes full of tears you look at the immigrant families
They believe in God they pray the women nurse their babies
They fill the Gare St. Lazare with their smell
Their faith in the stars rivals that of the three magi
They're hoping to gain some *argent* in the Argentine
And return to the old country with a fortune
One family takes a red eiderdown with it as you take your heart
          wherever you go
This eiderdown and our dreams are equally unreal
Some refugees stay in furnished rooms
In the rue des Rosiers or the rue des Écouffes in the slums
I have seen them at night walking
Like pieces on a chessboard they rarely move
Especially the Jews whose wives wear wigs
And sit quietly in the back of the shop

You stand at the counter of a seedy café
A cup of coffee for a couple of *sous* with the other outcasts

At night you go to a famous restaurant
These women aren't cruel they're just wretched
Each even the ugliest has made her lover suffer

She is the daughter of a policeman from Jersey

I hadn't noticed the calluses on her hand

I feel sorry for her and the scars on her belly

I humble my mouth to the poor girl with the horrid laugh

You're alone day breaks
The milkmen clink their bottles

The night slinks away like a half-breed beauty
Ferdine the false Leah on the lookout

The brandy you sip burns like your life
Your life that you drink like an *eau-de-vie*

You are walking toward Auteuil you intend to walk the whole way home
To sleep with your fetishes from Oceania and Guinea
There are Christs in different forms and other systems of belief
But Christs all the same though lesser though obscure

Farewell farewell

Let the sun beheaded be

Goethe's Nightsong

—*Wandrers Nachtlied* (1780)

Over the hills
Comes the quiet.
Across the treetops
No breeze blows.
Not a sound: even the small
Birds in the woods are quiet.
Just wait: soon you
Will be quiet, too.

Cento: The True Romantics

I hid my love when young till I
Heard the thunder hoarsely laugh,
Heard the skylark warbling in the sky,
For the eye altering alters all.

But with a sweet forgetting,
And a heaven in a wild flower,
The awful shadow of some unseen power
Hath had elsewhere its setting.

I would build that dome in air
And in the icy silence of the tomb,
For the sword outwears its sheath,

And whom I love, I love indeed,
And all I loved, I loved alone,
Ignorant and wanton as the dawn.

II

Selected Poems, 1974–2009

from *Yeshiva Boys* (2009)

On Purpose

"What is the purpose of your poems?"
I'm glad you asked me that
as I stand here in Mr. Ferry's eleventh-grade English class
in Lake Forest High School
I have given a lot of thought to "purpose"
Walking with a purposeful air in New York City
has obvious benefits in the chill of the night with wind
and it's even better when it's no bluff
you do know where you're going
from day to day
and you know when it's over
so it's like a story with a beginning middle and end
yet you could not tell me the purpose
of high school humiliation and I could not tell you
the purpose of this dream where you get up from these desks
and go to college and become lawyers or failures or soccer moms
and when you wake up you will have no recollection
of this encounter in the dark but it will linger nevertheless
and bring refreshment to your soul

Confessions of a Mask

These are the confessions of a mask.
I looked in the mirror and saw a ghost.
Of all lost causes I miss this one the most.
These are the questions you must not ask.

These are the oaks that once stood here.
And shall the earth be all of paradise
That we will know? Roll the dice;
These are the nights when praise turns into fear.

These are the memories of a man without a past.
Oh, I kept the first for another day!
Therefore, let us sport us while we may.
These are the reveries of a man who climbed the mast.

These are the reasons the student failed the course.
Some mute inglorious Milton
Against windmills did go tilting.
These are the seasons of a girl and her horse.

These are the days of sunlight and high skies.
Did she put on his knowledge with his power?
Unseal the earth and lift love in her shower.
These are the ways the humble man is wise.

These are the questions you must not ask.
Was it a vision or a waking dream?
Let be be finale of seem.
These are the confessions of a mask.

Homily

Man has the will
to grieve
a week and no longer.

Ever the stranger
he will kill
with righteous anger.

What does he believe?
In his right to trade
a season of greed

for an hour
of love in an unlit corner.
Such is love's power,

though it last no longer.
And such is his need
than which nothing is stronger.

The Real Thing

I don't agree
that dancing solves anything
except how to differentiate
between poetry and prose
the former being to the dance
(gratuitous)
what the latter is to taking a walk
(purposive)
according to Paul Valéry,
who felt that an artificial rose
was equal to or better than
the real thing.

I love that phrase: "The Real Thing."
It makes me think
of Henry James's story of that title
and the Coca-Cola commercial
identifying Coke as "the real thing."
If I could write an essay on that unusual
conjunction of names and facts
in fifteen minutes, it's because
you can do a lot in fifteen minutes
such as wash your hands, change the CD
from Anita O'Day to Dinah Shore singing
"Buttons and Bows," and write twenty-five
lines, which for some writers equals their entire
daily allotment. Or you can dance.

The other day I discovered the beginning
of a poem from 1980 handwritten
on a piece of paper tucked into my copy
of William Gass's *On Being Blue*.
The epigraph was from Rilke:
"Dance the Orange."
There are a couple of lines worth saving:
"Dance the skeleton on the doctor's desk."
"Dance the rabbi on one foot explaining the law."

Nevertheless I insist that
James Brown to the contrary notwithstanding
there's no point to it, nothing to gain from dancing,
and that is the great glory of the dance
though some might argue that dance
does have a purpose as the first step
toward mating and the reproduction of the species,
a complicated subject demanding more
than fifteen minutes, but as Ira Gershwin
wrote, I'm dancing and I can't
be bothered now.

Election Day

E. B. White said democracy
is a letter to the editor and
I'm not sure I agree though I
love letters to the editor
particularly loony ones that
begin by quoting Bob Dylan's
"Like a Rolling Stone" and end
by endorsing "nobody" for
president ("If nobody wins
nobody loses") but when I
think of democracy in America
I think not of Tocqueville but
of *The Great McGinty*
where the big city hero now
a bartender recounts how
he, a bum, got paid to vote early,
vote often, and so impressed
the machine boss that he rose
to become an alderman
then the mayor of the city
then governor and would have
kept the job, too, if he hadn't
(thanks to do-gooder wife)
tried to do some good for
the people some think
the moral is that politics
is crooked but I think it's
that anyone can grow up
to become governor

Money

It's money that puts the fannies in the seats.
It's money that pays the bills,
Buys the drinks, pays for the pills,
Separates the good guys from the cheats.

It's money that put the monkey on my back,
It's money that can make my monkey fly.
Money is unsentimental and never needs to lie.
Money is only that which we lack.

How to say this? Money is tits,
You either have them or you don't.
Money doesn't care if you will or if you won't.
For money never calls it quits.

For money's the honey that makes the babe talk
Money's the bunny that sat in my lap
Money's the flower that shut like a trap
Money's no dummy that makes the babe walk.

It's money for me and me for you,
It's what we do after we screw,
If false to you, to none can it be true,
It's you for me and money for you.

For money's the color of my true love's hair,
Money's the smell of her in the dark.
In the foreign night where no dogs bark,
Money's the flashlight that leads to her lair.

L'Shana Tova

for David Shapiro

I hear the ram's horn.
Do you? Do you remember
father, son, mountain?

L'shana tova
old friend, mentor, fellow Jew,
you from New Jersey,

I from Manhattan,
and we met not in temple
but Columbia

and do you recall
when I visited Cambridge
I left you a note

with the Clare porter.
The world is charged (I wrote) with
the grandeur of you!

And then you came home
and I took your place over
there: at Clare College

Peter Ackroyd came
and asked me if I would speak
to the group on John

Ashbery whose new
book *The Double Dream of Spring*
had just been published.

How could I say no?
They told me you had spoken
on Frank O'Hara

and Aaron Fogel
had spoken on Kenneth Koch.
It was a good omen

I thought but then what
happened was rain rain rain and
more rain. And no mail

because of a strike
in England. There was always
a strike in England.

No mail, no phone calls
to America where my
father lay dying.

The gardeners burned
the leaves and I crossed the Cam
on Clare College bridge

daily, and daily
I went to Heffer's and bought
books by Hölderlin,

Mann, Gide, Henry James.
I imitated Rilke.
The sonnet for you

ran in *Poetry.*
More rain. Cold toilet. Bad smell.
And I couldn't find

an English poet
younger than Larkin to like.
No mail. Pub hours.

Beer better than wine.
Awful food. Always hungry.
Had to learn to cook.

And that's where I went
—to the sea of memory—
in temple today

when I heard the sound
of the *shofar* and prayed for
the living and dead.

Paris, 1971

In retrospect it was romantic to be the lonely American recovering from pneumonia, living in a hotel room with a typewriter and a sink in a Left Bank hotel in a gray Paris winter.

At the time I was constantly cold, it rained seven days a week, my feet were wet, I was awkward with girls and wanted sex so badly I couldn't sleep at night, in London.

In retrospect I was neither Alyosha nor Ivan, not Orwell in Spain nor Hemingway on a fishing trip nor Henry Miller in Clichy.

At the time I saw *The Wild Bunch*, Sergio Leone's *Duck, You Sucker*, *The Go-Between*, *Sunday, Bloody Sunday*, and *Woodstock*.

In retrospect the gloom of the deserted streets and the sound of footfalls were full of strangeness in medieval Cambridge.

At the time I became self-conscious about my American accent. I began pronouncing the *t*'s in words like "city" or "university," and I said to-mah-to at the greengrocer's.

In retrospect I spent more money than my friends did at restaurants like the Koh-I-Noor, the Gardenia on Rose Crescent, and the Rembrandt. Then I learned to cook.

At the time I went to London for the weekend. There was a new place called the Great American Disaster that specialized in hamburgers. I saw John Gielgud in a matinee.

In retrospect I met a Swedish woman named Eva, blonde and beautiful, and the sex was great but we had nothing to talk about and I grew melancholy in the Scandinavian manner.

At the time I moved into an apartment near the rue des Écoles with a dandy who had a magnificent cane and liked walking with me to Montparnasse where a couple of Chaplin films were showing.

In retrospect I read "Le Cimetière marin" by Paul Valéry.

At the time I was a naïve American in a trench coat and fedora trying to make ends meet in Berlin in the waning days of the Weimar Republic.

In retrospect Beckett and Lorca.

At the time Stravinsky and Frank Zappa.

In retrospect Otto Dix, André Derain, and the Ballets suédois.

At the time the Pompes Funèbres sign between Saint Sulpice and Saint-Placide.

In retrospect we spent hours in the Rond-Point café playing Dipsy Doodle and other pinball machines made by the U.S. manufacturer Williams.

At the time steak tartare with capers and cornichons at Le Drugstore. I was sick for two days after.

In retrospect we went to Le Dôme, La Rotonde, Le Select, La Coupole, and the best of these was Le Dôme.

At the time Nicole asked me to find out whether she could come to England to have an abortion. She was my friend, not my girlfriend. I wasn't responsible.

In retrospect, the English doctor gave me as dirty a look as I've ever faced.

At the time of the Ali–Frazier fight at the Garden a smell like that of peaches wafted in the air, and spring was only weeks away.

In retrospect the Opéra, the Madeleine, the Sainte Chapelle, the Sacré Coeur, the Saint Germain.

At the time the Jockey Club where Lew played piano and we cheered him on—Gail and I and Tim and maybe even Edda.

In retrospect I visited Paul Auster in a garret near the Louvre, which he got with the help of Jacques Dupin.

At the time I read Simenon in French and (on Auster's recommendation) *The Real Life of Sebastian Knight*. He gave me a copy of his poem "Stele," and Larry Joseph filched it.

In retrospect I began a poem entitled "Interrupted Messages" and left it on my desk. Jonathan Lear came by when I wasn't in and wrote a note on the poem ending in the hope that he hadn't "sullied a vital piece of paper." I liked "sullied."

At the time the blue airmail letter summoning me to my father's deathbed arrived on a Tuesday morning. The in-flight movie on the way home was *Love Story*. I didn't see it. The off-duty flight attendant sitting next to me was engaged to be married to a minor league shortstop from Broken Arrow, Oklahoma.

In retrospect I took French lessons at the Alliance Française and went with a Spanish girl to a movie with Jean Gabin and Simone Signoret as an old quarrelsome married couple.

At the time I watched the little kids sail their toy boats in the Jardin du Luxembourg.

In retrospect I was always alone.

At the time I sat with you in the Bois de Boulogne and we took turns guessing what was in the mind of each person passing by.

French Movie

I was in a French movie
and had only nine hours to live
and I knew it
not because I planned to take my life
or swallowed a lethal but slow-working
potion meant for a juror
in a mob-related murder trial,
nor did I expect to be assassinated
like a chemical engineer mistaken
for someone important in Milan
or a Jew journalist kidnapped in Pakistan;
no, none of that; no grounds for
suspicion, no murderous plots
centering on me with cryptic phone
messages and clues like a scarf or
lipstick left in the front seat of a car;
and yet I knew I would die
by the end of that day
and I knew it with a dreadful certainty,
and when I walked in the street
and looked in the eyes of the woman
walking toward me I knew that
she knew it, too,
and though I had never seen her before,
I knew she would spend the rest of that day
with me, those nine hours walking,
searching, going into a bookstore in Rome,

smoking a Gitane, and walking,
walking in London, taking the train
to Oxford from Paddington or Cambridge
from Liverpool Street and walking
along the river and across the bridges,
walking, talking, until my nine hours
were up and the black-and-white movie
ended with the single word *FIN*
in big white letters on a bare black screen.

Desolation Row

The eccentric genius went crazy living by himself.
Few things held his attention.
Spy novels, baseball games on television, Japanese poetry, himself—
the things that used to gladden him now seemed flat or stale.
He felt like Wordsworth, gloomy on a sunny day.
There was a dinner one night. Coleridge sat at one end
of the table and Wordsworth at the other.
Both were talking about poetry. Coleridge was talking
excitedly about a Wordsworth poem. So was Wordsworth.
It was no fun feeling like Wordsworth.
He'd take Coleridge any day lamenting the theft
of his opiated genius by abstruse German philosophy.
"Deprivation is for me what daffodils were for Wordsworth,"
Philip Larkin quipped. But he knew better. There was
only one thing that held his interest now, and that was pornography.
This was after disillusion with the French Revolution
had set in. He thought maybe here was a subject
he could contemplate: disillusionment. Yes,
that's what he would do, that would be
his new project to ward off ennui.

Yeshiva Boys

1. The Ten Plagues

Came the plagues and we named them in order:
blood, frogs, lice, wild animals, pestilence, boils, hail,
locusts, darkness, and the slaying of the first born.

The scholars agree that hail was,
except for the slaying of the first born,
the most devastating of the ten.

Yet Pharaoh did not relent,
and the Egyptians knew not Joseph,
and God did not repent of his work.

The boys made the transition from Genesis
to Exodus when the infant Moses burned his tongue
on hot coals and spoke thereafter with a stammer.

All of a sudden there was a funny smell
that probably came from outside the room.
Since you all say it came from outside,

I shall assume that it came from within,
said Rabbi Kafka. The logic was unassailable
but what caused the smell that made the boys laugh?

If the *chutzpadik* does not stand up now,
you will all suffer, I can promise you that.
He folded his hands. We have ways of making you talk.

2. Rabbi Kafka

Rabbi Kafka asked the class whether the absence
of God dealt a fatal blow to religion.
If God is dead, is everything permitted?

Kalman Kurtz, the butcher's son, spoke first.
"Isn't it the other way around?" he asked.
"God is dead, because everything is permitted."

The boys in the back row traded baseball cards and
cigarettes and first day covers. Joshua Freundlich, who had old parents
and was the first among us to wear glasses, raised his hand:

"It's Nietzsche's fault." Not that God was dead but
morality was a hoax hatched by hook-nosed Jews,
the Jew as ugly Socrates, the weakling with the brain

who killed tragedy as surely as Plato expelled the poets
from the Republic. "The Nazis went where Nietzsche pointed:
a land beyond good and evil, during the twilight

of the idols." Reuben Ascher concurred. "For what is Fascism
but the glory of the all-conquering will, the rapist's conquest
of the anus?" Naftali Simon said: "They burned

the books. Action was language minus memory
and meaning, which is one reason Hitler resolved
never to write a thing down if he could say it."

Ephraim Menashe argued that the idea at the core
of Fascism is nihilism. "Then you're at sea and at the mercy
of any lifeboat that comes along." But Ezra Nehemiah interrupted.

"It's Heidegger's fault," he said, and would have said more if not for
the laughter that broke out from the back row of Rabbi Kafka's class.
One boy stood up. He said his name was Philip Roth and his fly

was open. "It's Rabbi Kafka's fault," he said. Then he walked
to the blackboard and erased it. Pandemonium. The very word
brought to mind a congress of devils at a war conference in hell.

In the commotion Kafka seized his chance to slip away.
*Let the starving artist make a virtue of his need: Let him fast.
That is his art.* And thus Kafka's Hunger Artist was born.

Crowds at his cage in the carnival
admired him. "But you shouldn't admire me,"
he said, dying. "And why shouldn't we?"

"Because I could never find the food that I liked!
If I had, I'd have stuffed my face like you and everyone else."
What a fellow he was! The attendant tossed a steak

to the panther in the next cage, in whose jaws
and flashing teeth you could see the essence of freedom,
while the hero, expiring, was only submitting to necessity.

Rabbi Kafka escaped to Mexico. Details are sketchy.
And Philip Roth died young, a sailor
in the battle of Okinawa in 1945.

3. This Be the Bread

The exodus from Egypt
took place again last night
This is the bread

of affliction this the wine
like the waters of the Red Sea parting
to let the people go

76

and they went to diverse places
each with a mark on his forehead
like the mark of Cain, progenitor

of the race, an invisible sign by which gentiles
the world over would recognize
the wandering *juif* without his yellow star

always the same story we prayed we fasted
we put on our prayer shawls and phylacteries
and got beaten up by the *goyim*

and then we went to Lodz
which became the largest
Jewish ghetto in Europe

and is now the largest Jewish
graveyard in Europe but
when we arrived the gates

were shut so we went
to the Holocaust memorial
the shape of an oven

deserted except for a couple
of kids smoking and necking
and we went inside and walked

down corridors of statistics
and photographs on the walls
born 1938 died 1943

terminating in a yard
of railway tracks a platform
and cattle car to Auschwitz

4. After Auschwitz

In the yeshiva playground they were marching
chanting marching around in circles bearing pickets
bearing scrolls saying "No poems after Auschwitz! No poems

about Auschwitz!" while in the back row
the poet sat dreamily and stared out the window, hungry.
Could there be lunch after Auschwitz?

His mother did everything she could have done
but there wasn't money enough for the necessary bribes
and her parents were deported to Riga and shot.

A woman he met at a writer's conference
told him she was working on *The Holocaust and Memory*
at Yale. The question she had was this:

Are American Jews making a fetish out of the Holocaust?
Has the Holocaust become the whole of Jewish experience?
"You go to shul on Yom Kippur or Passover

and everything is the Holocaust." I shut my eyes and hear
the old prayers made new: *"Shame is real," said Ida Noise.*
Hear, O Israel. The Lord is One. I, an American, naturally preferred

a temple carved out of water and stone: the rage of a waterfall,
the melody of a brook. But back-to-nature as a strategy failed
when the phones started ringing in the woods,

and only a child would think of collecting dead leaves
and trying to paste them back on the trees. So I returned
to the city, married, settled down, had a child of my own,

pretended that I was just like anybody else.
Yet I feel as if my real life is somewhere else, I left it
back in 1938, it happened already and yet it's still going on,

only it's going on without me, I'm merely an observer
in a trench coat, and if there were some way I could enter
the newsreel of rain that is Europe, some way I could return

to the year where I left my life behind,
it would be dear enough to me, danger and all. *To him,*
an emissary of a foreign war, London was unreal. He wondered

which of his fellow passengers would make the attempt.
He knew now that they would try to kill him,
tomorrow if not today. How could he have been such a fool?

Herr Endlich said: "We have our ways of making a man talk."
In the last forty-eight hours he had learned two things:
That you couldn't escape the danger, it was all around you,

and that the person who betrays you is the one you trusted most.
The strategists in Washington couldn't figure it out. Why in hell
were the Germans wasting fuel on trains to camps in Poland?

5. Sabbath Feast

How beautiful to me are the red fire escapes of my youth.

How goodly to me are the tents of morning housing the tenants of
dry seasons in books read and reread until mastered in old age by tigers
who crouch at the edge of the jungle ready to pounce.

How happy the wife who prepares the Sabbath feast.

How happy the son who knows by heart the benediction following
the meal.

How happy the daughters who recite the verses of the Bible for
their father's pleasure. This week Jacob wrestles the angel of God to a
standstill.

How purple the stain of the wine on the white tablecloth, how sweet
the ruby wine, how cool the taste on the lips and tongue, how full of
zest the grape as it bursts into life in the mouth.

How savory with salt the yellow bread, broken into pieces and
blessed, and eaten standing up.

How sweet to the man are the days of his youth. How surprised he would be, could he hear his own voice clamoring for attention at the dinner table with his parents and sisters and perhaps an uncle and aunt on a Friday night in 1961.

6. Intelligence

It's at this point in the picture that the man laughs
and says to the woman, *Go ahead, pull the trigger.*
You'll be doing me a favor. But she can't. She loves him

too much. There's a surprise ending,
but it's the same surprise they used the last time.
The butler did it: in this case, a book editor named Judith Butler.

Days of 1971. The railway stations looked like cathedrals
and though people said Europe had changed in outward ways,
Spain was still fascist and Vienna still full of Nazis.

How long ago it seems. I missed New York terribly,
though I had learned to love the fog of London in which
you could disappear into your anxiety and no one

would notice. I had a very good cover as a fellowship student
in comparative literature at Cambridge, and few guessed
the true nature of my employment in those years when

the Cold War was still frigid. I was in the Culture
Department. The French Resistance was something
we had cooked up to make the French feel less shame.

We came up with theories. *It was religion that made it easy to sin.*
Or: *The path to her panties was lubricated with gin.*
Or: *The Cold War was something we could win.*

In a shabby office near the Luxembourg Gardens
sat Rodgers, a blond man in his thirties
who had gone to Princeton and recruited me.

I reported on the growing hostility
of young French intellectuals
to Israel. Jews who opposed Israel were OK.

They're bitching about us left and right.
The French right can't stand Jimmy Carter.
Some crank out there is writing

that the Holocaust never happened
and the left is getting ready to defend him
on freedom-of-speech grounds.

A lot of sentences began, "You Americans."
You Americans are like California babes
with a clitoris where the mind should be.

You Americans with your loud stupid voices
are too soft or too innocent or too ignorant
or all three. You have a lesson coming to you.

But we knew better, savoring our melon with port.
"All painting," said Renoir, "is in the pink ribbon
on the dress of the Infanta." The nights were short,

and there was always time for one more drink. Everyone
had a part to play, and when the fistfight broke out at the pub,
I was the American, derided by all, trying to make peace between

the feuding Europeans. So years went by. In intelligence work
you learn to be tolerant of most people who lead
delusional lives, being unaware of the secret

you carry like a code or a dead language, and
that will die with you because you never revealed it
in all the pages you typed in hotel rooms in Europe.

7. The Categorical Imperative

But then we returned to the present
where Reb Gamliel, known for his strictness,
would examine each of us in turn solo in

his chambers with Reb Nachbar on hand to smile
encouragingly at each bewildered boy asked to parse
a sentence from the Talmud. My sentence concerned

Hillel's questions about biblical proscriptions and whether
the decree against murder applied in the case of an oppressor,
an executioner or assassin. "And what do *you* think?"

Reb Gamliel asked me gravely. And I, who had opinions
about everything, said, "Look at the uprising
in the Warsaw Ghetto. They had to fight, for

isn't it better to die in battle than be herded off in boxcars,
to be starved and beaten and finally gassed and burned?"
By this they knew I wasn't long for the yeshiva.

The two rabbis looked at each other with faint smiles.
And when they ushered me out of the room with
congratulatory handshakes and the promise of a high mark,

I was not deceived. I knew my future lay elsewhere
and I let it come rushing at me as an unsuspecting motorist
lets the landscape advance, who sits behind the wheel

of a vehicle that would explode upon impact
with another if both were traveling at sixty-five miles per hour,
going in opposite directions, having left home at the same time.

8. Action Painting

Rabbi Greenberg advocated abstract painting.
Rabbi Rosenberg called it action painting
Rabbi Kline had us study Chinese calligraphy.

My next assignment was to explain
the enduring appeal of Communism
to Italian workers, French students, and English departments.

I don't get it, Rodgers said.
There's nothing more boring than Communism.
Communism means long lines for bread and longer ones for shoes.

What do they see in it?
The Red army let the Nazis raze Warsaw. Then they entered.
He stood at the curtain's edge and looked out the window.

Are you sure you weren't followed?
So I went to Munich, to Milan and to Rome.
Munich in '72 was Israel's first and gravest military defeat.

There's a new enemy.
You can call them terrorists, but then
you'd be defining them by their tactics

and leaving unstated the ideology
behind them. Was it nihilism
as in the anarchist days of Joseph Conrad's

The Secret Agent, or was there something
malignant and medieval on the horizon?
Langley was still fixated on the Soviets

the year the Americans were held hostage
in Teheran, and the Russians invaded Afghanistan.
The center of gravity was about to move

from Berlin to Jerusalem
from Marxism to Muslim fanaticism
and what are you going to do about it, paint an abstract canvas?

9. Safe House

The black seeds on the fresh pink watermelon
looked like flies, and biscotti were served.
The Turin gang was up to something. Rumors

circulated that the next wave of terror attacks
would involve the kidnapping of industrialists
and high-profile politicians whose ears

would fall victim to the executioner's shears
if an outlandish ransom weren't paid. I rented a room
from a schoolteacher in Padua where I'd gone

ostensibly for the Giottos, so blue, but in actuality because
the Turin gang's number two man was said to be
hiding out there. Nothing much happened. I had an affair

with the schoolteacher, who worked miracles in the kitchen
and was pretty, with brown bangs and dark brown eyes.
She had a four-year-old we would take to the park.

Once or twice I had the impulse to fabricate
an incident or a conspiracy in my monthly report.
The codes were elaborate and it took hours to send

even a simple message. For example, "the Colosseum
will be a handsome building when it's finished"
meant "no change," while "the meaner the convent cell,

the richer the convent chapel" translated as
"suspect Padua a bum steer."
Then one day they found Rodgers in his Paris office

with his throat slashed. I left Italy
for the safe house in Zurich where a face as grim
as mine poured brandy and ordered me back to Britain.

The worst was when I met his widow, but
it was a hell of a lot better than Tu Do Street in Saigon.
And what's more, I got to read the surrealists and write bad poems.

My mistress's eyes were almonds, her breasts
were apricots, and her shapely ass was a picnic basket
loaded with cheese, a baguette, and a bottle of wine.

10. The Red Death

Arthur Schopenhauer, Rabbi Biegeleisen's favorite student,
stood up and said he was awestruck at the power
of the will to live, the urge to mate,

despite the misery and pain of human existence.
And so Schopenhauer became known as a pessimist, though
it seems like good old-fashioned horse sense to me, said Beth Hayes.

And God said *Be frutiful and multiply.*
This was God's first command.
And just to sweeten the deal, you get to fornicate

like beasts but with the capacity to think about it
afterwards, in secret in the dark, with remembered pleasure
or shame or guilt or love of the one you have linked with.

Nihilism is dead as utopia is nowhere
and high school sucks but it's better than the old country.
You can always treat yourself to an existential crisis.

God made man in his own image, and man
instantly returned the favor. Did Voltaire say that?
And darkness moved upon the face of the waters.

Next door they were practicing. They had
simulated the camp down to the last detail,
the barbed wire that electrocuted you if you touched it.

And I stood hatless in the wind of the Lord
and saw from the mountaintop what the new year held.
And one by one dropped the revellers

in the blood-bedewed halls of their revel
and died each in the despairing posture of his fall.
And Darkness and Decay and the Red Death held illimitable
  dominion over all.

11. The Wrong Man

My Cambridge don waxed eloquent.
"As the *marabout* on his African dunghill
promises a *Mahdi* to the dejected Bedouin,

so the Jews of the diaspora embraced
mystical heresies, counted the days
to the Millennium, or discovered the Messiah."

I met her every Wednesday for a year.
How can you blame me for falling
in love with her? I still have a lock of her hair.

It was the year the Berlin Wall came down
and the Ayatollah issued his fatwah
targeting a blasphemous Muslim novelist.

The information I had could get me killed.
The Sunnis were bad enough
but this new bunch was something else again.

They felt they could terrorize Europe in ten
years, tops. Anti-Semitism is a beautiful thing,
said M. It can even exist without Jews.

They laughed. Fifty years after the Holocaust,
and charming rogue profs at Brown or Penn
quipped, "There's no business like Shoah business."

It took me a day and a half to decode the message,
a page torn out of a spy novel from an earlier era.
"You will be arrested at the Spanish Steps

on drug charges and held in jail for a year."
The waiting was terrible.
My contact turned up finally and led me

to a blue Fiat beside a ditch near a cement factory
with a body full of bullets in the boot.
"You bloody fool! You've killed the wrong man."

12. Preparing to Meet the Maker

The maker of paradoxes, asked to expose
his worst fears and ours, omits the roses
and stars and Spanish wars and guitars

on Venetian balconies. Instead of an epiphany,
he offers the heightened sense of perplexity
that hunger artists have wished on us in pity,

and we love them for it, before dying
in their arms, like a chastened Cordelia, crying—
but with her innocence intact. Asked to expose

the secret agenda of our nightmares, the boy
in the back row says everything's up for grabs,
negotiable, "on the table," but first we must decide

the shape of the table, and time is running out.
He has a sense of humor, and a headache.
He never got over the problem of evil, the problem of

the philosopher's brown shirt, and the irrational
nostalgia a man of forty feels for his childhood,
which was full of torment at the time.

To those who phone him, asking for a quote,
the maker of paradoxes is unfailingly polite.
He knows there is nothing else he can do.

Epilogue

"When I was born the third child to my parents, they were not overjoyed, since they already had a daughter and a son. But my mother told me I was so pretty that they didn't mind too much.

"We lived in Vienna in the 16th district. It was not a very Jewish district. Jews lived mostly in the 2nd and 20th districts. And in my class in school were only three Jewish girls out of thirty students. Of course from an early time we were made to feel different. Yet I had many gentile girlfriends and I remember one of them I was pretty close to. Her parents had a little garden with a hut in the outskirts of Vienna and she invited me to sleep over. Yet when Hitler came to power and I met her on the street, she acted funny and held her hand over her bosom until I found out she was wearing a swastika! This was years before Hitler overran Austria—she must have been an underground member in order to have the swastika. This gave me a real shock.

"The police came one day and asked for Adolf. They had orders to take him to the police station. Why, we asked. We need him as a witness, they said. He was present at an accident, they said. We told them: as soon as he comes home we shall send him to the police station. But of course when Adolf came home he told us there had been no accident. He was on a list. The Nazis wanted to send him to a camp. You see, Adolf was the president of some idealistic university organization, a good socialist. And from that day on, he went underground until he got a visa to go to America.

"It was a nightmare to live in Vienna at that time. Every time the doorbell rang, we were afraid—*they're coming for us!*

89

"A friend of mine got me a permit to go to England as a mother's helper. This way I got out of Nazi Germany. These people, Wright was their name, lived in Southsea. He was a shipbuilder and she was a dentist. They treated me very well, and he gave me English lessons every day. But I was lonely there, so after a few months I went to London, where I had some friends from Vienna. My friend Trude and I found work in the home of an English theatre producer by the name of French. Trude was supposed to be the cook and I was the parlor maid. Once Rex Harrison came to dinner. He was very friendly, a real gentleman.

"I was in England when the war started and we all received the gas masks and instructions for the air raid shelters. The American consulate closed and we had to move to a refugee home. When I saw how bad the situation was and my parents were still in Vienna, I tried to get them out to England. For America they had to wait too long, their quota was very small, since my parents were born in Poland. And we did not know when Hitler came how important it was to be registered in the American consulate. In March 1938 Adolf went to register himself and in April Bert went. I only went in June to register, but at least while I was there I also got the papers to register my parents. Later I found out that each month meant one more year to wait for the visa. But it took even longer if you were born in Poland. So I asked the French people and they filled out a lot of papers which would have enabled my parents to come to England. Everything took so long, when I finally got everything together England was at war and my parents couldn't come. I had no way of getting in touch with them.

"But the American consulate finally opened its door again and I received my visa to go to America. How happy I was. Naturally I was worried to travel on an English ship, so my cousin from America sent me additional money and I changed my ticket to an American ship, the *President Harding*. I think it was the last Atlantic crossing it ever made. It took us ten days of the most terrible shaking. Everyone on board was sick and wanted to die. We were so sick that we weren't even afraid of hidden mines, and as in a dream we did all the safe drillings, etc. The last day was Thanksgiving. We had, and for me it was the first time, a delicious Thanksgiving dinner with turkey and all the trimmings, they played 'Oh, say, can you see,' and when I finally saw the Statue of Liberty, I was really grateful to God, that he let me live and see America."

from *When a Woman*

Loves a Man (2005)

The Magician

The magician was a soulful man, quick rather than deep.
He always gave you the feeling that he knew more
than he was letting on about the audience and how
tempting it had been to bend them to his will,
though he didn't—he would rather absent himself
than play the poor man's Mussolini. So he took off,
not often but a lot, staying away just long enough to make
his reappearance go unremarked. He spent months
preparing for each transition, switching identities
with wigs and false noses. He wanted to be known
by no one but the dog walking beside him into the woods,
where a No Swimming sign means you can be pretty sure
people are swimming. Old conversations replayed themselves
in his mind. Every third sentence began "To be honest
with you," suggesting a general rule of falsehood.
The past was a hotel. The room was empty. The door
was open. He stepped in the door. There was no door.

In Freud's House

1.

I met Freud in the locker room after red-haired
Mrs. Kelly who taught English walked in the door
and blushed, and the boys cheered except for Freud and me.
Thus began our friendship of forty-eight years.
The first thing I would say about him is,
he always appreciated a good cigar. He wrote
an ode to his cigar to which he felt he owed
his "tenacity and self-control" (I quote).

2.

A copy of Ingres' *Oedipus and the Sphinx*
hung on the wall at 19 Berggasse in Vienna
where, in September 1891, he began seeing patients.
I saw him there. He explained his system to me once.
The organization of the personality was a science
that worked like a myth. Each man was the naked
infant Cupid but also the cop on the beat
and the driver of a parked car asleep at the wheel.

3.

Nabokov joked: "Schadenfreude means hatred of Freud."
But they loved him on Broadway. He knew that jokes
were a way to recover the mood we had as children,
"when we didn't need humor to make us feel happy."
His name means Joy in German. This pleased him. Much
has been made of his use of cocaine, which he regarded
as a good local anesthetic, though his enthusiasm for it waned.
He was happiest with his dogs and cigars in rented summer houses.

4.

Each word was its own antonym, each object
a symbol like a drawing of a man smoking a cigar
with the legend "this is not a cigar." Sometimes we smoked
together in the gloaming. He told me the hero of his youth
was Hannibal, who symbolized "the tenacity of Jewry"
against Rome, which stood for the Catholic church.
He told me he needed to be alone but put his hand
on my shoulder so as not to hurt my feelings.

5.

He needed his solitude if he was going to work like
Marat saving the Revolution or Zola arguing for Dreyfus.
On his door he put up a homely little sign saying *Enfin seul*
but took it down because no one would be there to admire it.
He was thirty-five that year, 1891. He felt that he and Martha
could stand as a model for future generations of lovers, because
they "had the courage to become fond of each other without
asking anyone's permission." What progress we have made.

6.

The Nazis burned his books. "What progress we have made.
In the Middle Ages they would have burned me.
Now they are content with burning my books."
It seemed that humanity as a whole, in its development
through the ages, fell into states analogous to neuroses,
and every individual was the enemy of civilization,
and every civilization was built on coercion,
and every dream was a jail cell with a ladder and a window.

7.

"Life at Bellevue is turning out very pleasantly
for everyone," he told me. "The wild roses are in bloom,
the scent of acacia and jasmine has succeeded that of lilac
and viburnum, and everything, as even I notice,
seems to have burst into flower. Do you suppose
some day someone will place a marble tablet here:
'In this house on July 24, 1895, the secret of dreams was
revealed to Dr. Sigmund Freud'?" Then he laughed, a regular guy.

The Human Factor

The gambler knows nothing's
more addictive than deception
with the chance that the betrayed one,
the spouse or the State, is pretending
or consenting to be deceived
for motives of vanity and greed
not different from his own,
leaving him with a choice to make
between his mistress and his self-respect—
which may be why the ideal reader
of Graham Greene's novels went
to a parochial school, was married
and divorced, has lived abroad
in Europe or Asia, plays in a weekly
small-stakes poker game, works
for a newspaper, lies to make a living.

Who He Was

He walked fast. Anyone watching
would think he knew where he was going.

He lived alone.
The small shocks of everyday life
bummed him out. His phone
went dead for the second time in a week
on account of the phone company
changing technologies
from copper to fiber optic.

One year he wanted a chemistry set
for his birthday. The next year
a camera. Then a stereo so he could
listen to Bob Dylan sing I ain't
gonna work on Maggie's farm no more.

He wrote a story about
a man living in the Upper West Side
whose next-door neighbor,
a beautiful art historian at Barnard,
is murdered for unknown reasons.

Luckily, when his next-door neighbors were found
with their throats slashed,
he was a junior at Columbia driving

from Cleveland to Columbus
(he saw how big America was).

The key to happiness lay in being
the only citizen who didn't watch
the O.J. trial or Princess Di's death
or even the Gulf War on TV.
He was too busy reading John Cheever's journals.

The interviewer asked if he could give an example
of a preposterous lie that tells the truth about life
and Cheever said "the vows of holy matrimony"
without hesitation and at night while the neighbors slept
he became the housebreaker of Shady Hill
who had read his Kierkegaard, and knew,

"When two people fall in love and begin to feel
that they're made for one another, then it's time
for them to break off, for by going on they have
everything to lose and nothing to gain."

She met him at a party. He was holding two drinks.
She laughed, and he gave her one of them.

She met him at the door. "You don't look
like a rapist," she smiled.

She wondered why he was late,
why was he always late? He doesn't phone. Why
doesn't he phone? What's he doing
with the light on in the attic at three in the morning?

There were things that scared him: blood tests, catheters.

He was a Gemini with Leo rising
and with Mercury and Venus in Cancer.

She saw him when he wasn't there.
She came over to listen to Chet Baker sing
"I'm Old-Fashioned." She listened
and said, "Oh that, that's heroin music."

In business school he wrote a paper
on one of the most lucrative sentences
of the late twentieth century:
"Would you like fries with that?"

He had the voice of a man whose greatest accomplishment
was that he made it onto Nixon's enemies list.
"I used to think there was a right way
and a wrong way to do everything
Now I know there's only one way,"
he said whistling as he left, a Wall Street expert.
"When they shoot the generals it means
the war is nearly over," he grinned (he was always leaving
that's what she remembered him doing
that's what he did best) and didn't turn around
when he walked out the door.

Dante Lucked Out

T. S. Eliot held that Dante was lucky
to live in the Middle Ages
because life then was more logically organized
and society more coherent. The rest of us however
can't be as sure that if we'd had the fortune
to walk along the Arno and look at the pretty girls
walking with their mothers in the fourteenth century,
then we, too, would have composed *La Vita Nuova*
and the *Divine Comedy*. It is on the contrary
far more likely that we, transported
to medieval Florence, would have died miserably
in a skirmish between the Guelphs and the Ghibellines
without the benefit of anesthesia
or would have been beaten, taunted,
cheated, and cursed as usurers
two centuries before the charging of interest
became an accepted part of Calvinist creed
and other reasons needed to be produced
to justify the persecution of the Jews.

Radio

I left it
on when I
left the house
for the pleasure
of coming back
ten hours later
to the greatness
of Teddy Wilson
"After You've Gone"
on the piano
in the corner
of the bedroom
as I enter
in the dark

A History of Modern Poetry

The idea was to have a voice of your own,
distinctive, sounding like nobody else
The result was that everybody sounded alike
The new idea was to get rid of ideas
and substitute images especially the image
of a rock so everyone wrote a poem
with the image of a rock in it capped with snow
or unadorned this was in the 1970s
a decade before Pet Rocks were a Christmas craze
showing that poetry was ahead of its time as usual
and poetry had moved on
the new idea was to make language the subject
because language was an interference pattern
there was no such thing as unmediated discourse
and the result was that everybody sounded alike

Like a Party

You throw a war and hope people will come.
They do, and they bring signs, they bring rifles,
They make speeches, they build bombs,
And they fight the last war, or protest its arrival.
But this is now. One myth of war is that it takes
A lot of careful planning. Bunk. All you need is a cake
With a roll of film inside, or a briefcase full of germs.
Another myth stars Vulcan the smith,
Limping husband of Venus, mistress of Mars,
Who says: The bully broke my nose and what was I
To do, cry in the corner and ask him why
He didn't like me, or punch him back harder than he
Hit me? The war was not a play, not a movie but a mess;
Not a work of art; and if a game of chess, blind chess.

Wittgenstein's Ladder

> My propositions serve as elucidations in the following way:
> anyone who understands me eventually recognises them as
> nonsensical, when he has used them—as steps—to climb up
> over them. (He must, so to speak, throw away the ladder
> after he has climbed up it.)
>
> —Ludwig Wittgenstein, *Tractatus*

1.

The first time I met Wittgenstein, I was
late. "The traffic was murder," I explained.
He spent the next forty-five minutes
analyzing this sentence. Then he was silent.
I wondered why he had chosen a water tower
for our meeting. I also wondered how
I would leave, since the ladder I had used
to climb up here had fallen to the ground.

2.

Wittgenstein served as a machine-gunner
in the Austrian Army in World War I.
Before the war he studied logic in Cambridge
with Bertrand Russell. Having inherited
his father's fortune (iron and steel), he

gave away his money, not to the poor, whom
it would corrupt, but to relations so rich
it would not thus affect them.

3.

He would visit Russell's rooms at midnight
and pace back and forth "like a caged tiger.
On arrival, he would announce that when
he left he would commit suicide. So, in spite
of getting sleepy, I did not like to turn him out." On
such a night, after hours of dead silence, Russell said,
"Wittgenstein, are you thinking about logic or about
your sins?" "Both," he said, and resumed his silence.

4.

On leave in Vienna in August 1918
he assembled his notebook entries
into the *Tractatus*. Certain it provided
the definitive solution to all the problems
of philosophy, he decided to broaden
his interests. He became a schoolteacher,
then a gardener's assistant at a monastery
near Vienna. He dabbled in architecture.

5.

He returned to Cambridge in 1929,
receiving his doctorate for the *Tractatus*,
"a work of genius," in G. E. Moore's opinion.
Starting in 1930 he gave a weekly lecture
and led a weekly discussion group. He spoke
without notes amid long periods of silence.

Afterwards, exhausted, he went to the movies
and sat in the front row. He liked Carmen Miranda.

6.

Philosophy was an activity, not a doctrine.
"Solipsism, when its implications are followed out
strictly, coincides with pure realism," he wrote.
Dozens of dons wondered what he meant. Asked
how he knew that "this color is red," he smiled
and said, "Because I have learnt English." There
were no other questions. Wittgenstein let the
silence gather. Then he said, "This itself is the answer."

7.

Religion went beyond the boundaries of language,
yet the impulse to run against "the walls of our cage,"
though "perfectly, absolutely useless," was not to be
dismissed. A. J. Ayer, one of Oxford's ablest minds,
was puzzled. If logic cannot prove a nonsensical
conclusion, why didn't Wittgenstein abandon it,
"along with the rest of metaphysics, as not worth
serious attention, except perhaps for sociologists"?

8.

Because God does not reveal himself in this world, and
"the value of this work," Wittgenstein wrote, "is that
it shows how little is achieved when these problems
are solved." When I quoted Gertrude Stein's line
about Oakland, "there is no there there," he nodded.
Was there a there, I persisted. His answer: Yes and No.
It was as impossible to feel another person's pain
as to suffer another person's toothache.

9.

At Cambridge the dons quoted him reverently.
I asked them what they thought was his biggest
contribution to philosophy. "Whereof one cannot
speak, thereof one must be silent," one said.
Others spoke of his conception of important
nonsense. But I liked best the answer John
Wisdom gave: "His asking of the question
'Can one play chess without the queen?'"

10.

Wittgenstein preferred American detective
stories to British philosophy. He liked lunch
and didn't care what it was, "so long as it was
always the same," noted Professor Malcolm
of Cornell, a former student, in whose house
in Ithaca Wittgenstein spent hours doing
handyman chores. He was happy then.
There was no need to say a word.

Anna K.

1.

Anna believed.
Couldn't delay.
Every Friday
grew heroic
infidelity just
knowing love
might never
otherwise present
queenly resplendent
satisfaction trapped
under Vronsky's
wild X-rated
young zap.

2.

Afraid. Betrayed.
Can't divorce.
Envy follows
grim heroine,
inks judgment,
kills lust.
Mercy nowhere.
Opulent pink

quintessence radiates
suicide trip—
unique vacation—
worst Xmas,
yesterday's zero.

Brooklyn Bridge

after Vladimir Mayakovsky

Hey, Coolidge,
                 shout for joy!
I've got to hand
               it to you—
with compliments
                     that will make you blush
                                 like my country's flag
no matter how United
                   States of America
                          you may be!
As a madman
             enters a church
or retreats
            to a monastery,
                     pure and austere,
so I,
      in the haze
               of evening
humbly approach
               the Brooklyn Bridge.
Like a conqueror
               with cannons
                   tall as giraffes

entering a besieged
                city, so, drunk
                        with glory,
higher than a kite,
              I cross
                  the Brooklyn Bridge.
Like a painter
            whose smitten eyes pierce
                        a museum Madonna
through the glass of a frame,
                  so I look at New York
                          through the Brooklyn Bridge
and see the sky and the stars.

New York,
          hot and humid
                  until night,
has now forgotten
              the daily fight,
                    and only the souls
of houses rise
            in the serene
                  sheen of windows.
Here the hum
            of the El
                can hardly be heard,
and only by this hum,
                soft but stubborn,
can you sense the trains
                crawling
                    with a rattle
as when dishes clatter
              in a cupboard.
And when from below,
              a merchant transports sugar
                      from the factory bins,

the masts
            passing under the bridge
                        are no bigger than pins.
I'm proud of just this
                mile of steel.
My living visions here
                stand tall:
a fight for structure over style,
                        the calculus of beams of steel.
If the end of the world should come,
                        wiping out the earth,
                                    and all that remains
is this bridge,
            then, as little bones, fine as needles,
                            are assembled into dinosaurs
in museums,
            so from this bridge
                        the geologists of the future
will reconstruct
                our present age.
                            They will say:
This paw of steel
                linked seas and prairies.
                            From here,
Europe rushed to the West, scattering
                        Indian feathers
                                    to the wind.
This rib
            reminds us of a machine—
                            imagine having the strength,
while standing
                with one steel leg
                        in Manhattan,
to pull Brooklyn
            toward you
                    by the lip!

By these cables and wires
                    I know we have retired
                                        the age of coal and steam.
Here people screamed
                    on the radio,
                                        or flew in planes.
For some life was a picnic;
                    for others a prolonged
                                        and hungry howl.
From here desperate men
                    jumped to their deaths
                                        in the river.
And finally I see—
                    Here stood Mayakovsky,
                                        composing verse, syllable by syllable.
I look at you
                    as an Eskimo admires a train.
I stick to you
                    as a tick to an ear.
Brooklyn Bridge,
                    you're really something, aren't you?

The Party of Ideas

Existentialism was there, smoking on the balcony.
Inside, Descartes' Cogito held a volume of Spinoza's *Ethics*
in one hand and a glass of port in the other as if the difference
between them were either self-evident or nonexistent.
The dictatorship of the proletariat had made eye contact
with the theory of infantile sexuality. Cardinal Newman
("The Idea of a University") chatted amiably if a bit stuffily with
the Sublime, who kept looking over his shoulder in the approved
manner of New Yorkers at parties on the lookout for someone
more important than the person they are speaking to,
only this was the party of ideas, where the idea of a republic, a democracy,
and the idea of the self-determination of nations could mingle
at the end of the day, satisfied. The idea that history repeats
itself was there. The idea that history repeats itself was there.
Logical Positivism was there, a kindly old pipe-smoking don who
asked you to his rooms for sherry and said he was cautiously optimistic.
The buzz in the room was that the first refuge of a scoundrel
had begun an affair with the last infirmity of noble mind,
which explained why neither of them was present. Art for
art's sake was there, nursing a vodka gimlet. It was clear
from a look at Utopia's face that she'd had one brandy Alexander
too many, but British empiricism looked none the worse for wear.
Everyone said so, especially American pragmatism, savoring
a new wrinkle. The Noble Savage tended bar.
The Categorical Imperative wouldn't take no for an answer.
I thought of "The Idea of Order at Key West" and took a leap of faith
opening a door hoping it led to the men's room.

The Prophet's Lantern

What's new?
The question implies a possibility:
that the old saw wasn't true,
the one that says there's nothing
new under the sun.
The prophet rests in the shade.

Not black but a dark shade
of blue is the shade in which the new
growth, protected from the sun,
tests the possibility
that the prophet's vision of nothing
could not come true.

The prophet knows true
north is the direction of a shade
after death when nothing
further can be done, no new
remedy can revive the possibility
of new light from an ancient sun.

In the glare of the midday sun
things that were true
at night grow faint. The possibility
of love's warmth in a cool shade
is what's needed: something new,
not just a reiteration of nothing.

"The sun shone on the nothing
new," he wrote. Blank was the sun,
the masses quit the church, and new
pigeons ate stale bread. The true
isn't equal to the good; there's a shade
of difference between the possibility

that judgment is futile and the possibility
that it can't be evaded, as nothing
in our destiny can be. Linger in the shade,
we may as well. We cannot bear too much sun
if the one thing that is true
is that everything is possible, nothing new.

Yet news travels fast. Nothing lasts.
The possibility of love among the shades
remains as true as when the sun was new.

The Code of Napoleon

It is not only true that Napoleon isn't crazy if he thinks
he is Napoleon; it is also true that Napoleon had to be a
little crazy to think he could become Napoleon. "All mortal
greatness is but disease," says Ahab.
—Quentin Anderson, *The Imperial Self*

1.

Napoleon never felt the need to remind people that he *was* Napoleon,
And in this way he differed from the legion of lunatics
Who say they are Napoleon, and can prove it.
You'll recognize the genuine article when you see him:
He's the shortest man in the room, the only one who thinks
He is Adolf Hitler. Everyone else is Napoleon.

2.

As a boy, Napoleon had an undersized body and an oversized head.
It kept him off balance. He got into fights.
"When I had the honor to be a second lieutenant," he said,
"I ate dry bread, but I never let anyone know I was poor."
Tolstoy spat. The Corsican was "a man of no convictions,
No habits, no traditions, no name, *not even a Frenchman*."

3.

Napoleon took power on the eighteenth day of the month
Of mists, Brumaire in the calendar of the Revolution.
He was the prime beneficiary of a coup d'état: the Council
Of Elders had banished parliament to St. Cloud
For its own safety, and handed Paris to Napoleon,
Who never secretly wondered whether he *was* Napoleon.

4.

Bonaparte conquered Italy in 1796. Two years later
The morale of his troops survived the calamities
Of Egypt: hunger and sickness, syphilis and bubonic plague.
From the summit of the pyramids, forty centuries looked down
Upon the victorious soldiers of Napoleon. Accused of betraying
The revolution, Napoleon said, "I *am* the French Revolution."

5.

According to Napoleon, a revolution was an opinion with bayonets.
In 1803 he considered a plan to invade England by balloon
And by tunneling beneath the English Channel. Was he mad?
Or was war not hell but life at its most vital, and peace
The bequest of the imperial will? Even skeptics saluted
The Napoleonic Code, a single legal system for all of Europe.

6.

On the other hand, consider the student in St. Petersburg
Who, thinking he was Napoleon, killed a pawnbroker. Wasn't
Hitler's invasion of Russia an act of brazen imitation?
Yet would I say a word for his ardor and ambition.
Nor will I forget the ten-year-old boy in military school
Taunted by the others: "the Little Corporal."

7.

Before Napoleon, the unkillable poor could aspire to
Nothing finer than prejudice and religious
Superstition allowed. You were what you were from birth.
No alteration in the hierarchy was tolerated.
It was the villains in Shakespeare who claimed
That men, not stars, held their destiny in their hands.

8.

He unified his foes, sold Louisiana to the United States,
Entered Russia with half a million men, the enemy in retreat,
Only to be beaten by hunger, his supply lines overextended;
Death, desertion, illness, a bad cold, a bladder infection.
When his army reached Moscow, it was a ghost city.
By November the temperature dropped to twenty degrees below zero.

9.

Napoleon failed, not because of his blundering generals but
Because ravens froze at midnight and fell to the ground
In midflight; the feet of the shoeless soldiers froze
Into useless clogs. Then came Elba, then Waterloo.
And the century so full of romantic fervor settled
Into an age of hypocrisy and pleasant vice.

10.

Because of him, country boys climbed ladders
Into the bed chambers of eminent men's wives
And ended up facing the executioner's mask
With Beethoven's *Eroica* booming in the background.
*"Talking to myself, two paces from death, I'm still
A hypocrite," he thought. "O nineteenth century!"*

The Gift

He gave her class. She gave him sex.
  —Katharine Hepburn on
    Fred Astaire and Ginger Rogers

He gave her money. She gave him head.

He gave her tips on "aggressive growth" mutual funds. She gave him a
    red rose and a little statue of eros.

He gave her Genesis 2 (21–23). She gave him Genesis 1 (26–28).

He gave her a square peg. She gave him a round hole.

He gave her Long Beach on a late Sunday in September. She gave him
    zinnias and cosmos in the plenitude of July.

He gave her a camisole and a brooch. She gave him a cover and a break.

He gave her Venice, Florida. She gave him Rome, New York.

He gave her a false sense of security. She gave him a true sense of
    uncertainty.

He gave her the finger. She gave him what for.

He gave her a black eye. She gave him a divorce.

He gave her a steak for her black eye. She gave him his money back.

He gave her what she had never had before. She gave him what he had
    had and lost.

He gave her nastiness in children. She gave him prudery in adults.

He gave her Panic Hill. She gave him Mirror Lake.

He gave her an anthology of drum solos. She gave him the rattle of
    leaves in the wind.

When a Woman Loves a Man

When she says margarita she means daiquiri.
When she says "quixotic" she means "mercurial."
And when she says, "I'll never speak to you again,"
she means, "Put your arms around me from behind
as I stand disconsolate at the window."

He's supposed to know that.

When a man loves a woman he is in New York and she is in Virginia
or he is in Boston, writing, and she is in New York, reading,
or she is wearing a sweater and sunglasses in Balboa Park and he
   is raking leaves in Ithaca
or he is driving to East Hampton and she is standing disconsolate
at the window overlooking the bay
where a regatta of many-colored sails is going on
while he is stuck in traffic on the Long Island Expressway.

When a woman loves a man it is one ten in the morning
she is asleep he is watching the ball scores and eating pretzels
drinking lemonade
and two hours later he wakes up and staggers into bed
where she remains asleep and very warm.

When she says tomorrow she means in three or four weeks.
When she says, "We're talking about me now,"
he stops talking. Her best friend comes over and says,
"Did somebody die?"

When a woman loves a man, they have gone
to swim naked in the stream
on a glorious July day
with the sound of the waterfall like a chuckle
of water rushing over smooth rocks,
and there is nothing alien in the universe.

Ripe apples fall about them.
What else can they do but eat?

When he says, "Ours is a transitional era,"
"that's very original of you," she replies,
dry as the martini he is sipping.

They fight all the time
It's fun
What do I owe you?
Let's start with an apology
OK, I'm sorry, you dickhead.
A sign is held up saying "Laughter."
It's a silent picture.
"I've been fucked without a kiss," she says,
"and you can quote me on that,"
which sounds great in an English accent.

One year they broke up seven times and threatened to do it
    another nine times.

When a woman loves a man, she wants him to meet her at the
    airport in a foreign country with a jeep.
When a man loves a woman he's there. He doesn't complain that
    she's two hours late
and there's nothing in the refrigerator.

When a woman loves a man, she wants to stay awake.
She's like a child crying
at nightfall because she didn't want the day to end.

When a man loves a woman, he watches her sleep, thinking:
as midnight to the moon is sleep to the beloved.
A thousand fireflies wink at him.
The frogs sound like the string section
of the orchestra warming up.
The stars dangle down like earrings the shape of grapes.

from *The Evening Sun:*

A Journal in Poetry (2002)

January 1

When Joe was five he didn't say I'm hungry
he said I feel the hungriness and later that late August day
the hottest in years he gathered the fallen leaves
and pasted them back on the trees I feel like that
today like Joe at five or the tourist in paradise whose
visa has expired the revolution has begun the junta
has shut down the airport there's no escape so here I'll say
goodbye to the other children I knew when we were
children, skating at the edge of the pond, I didn't specially
want it to happen, this change in the clock calendar century
I just wanted things to continue as they had, do I sound like
a jilted lover no you sound like yourself and I'm here I'm hearing
everything twice everything twice a saxophone a trumpet
and then a singer lifts me with soft lights and sweet music
and you in my arms let's be like the boy at five who
said he wanted to be a ghost when he grew up but
grew up to celebrate the marriage of flesh and air
in a lonely place with paranoid Bogart and Gloria
Grahame the director's wife that's poetry noir for you
champagne cocktails with blood orange juice and
then to eat with a hearty appetite feeling the hungriness

January 8

The wind does whistle but it also hums
if you say it does, because you have
that power: language makes it possible,
and you have the choice: you can revile

the slogans and shibboleths of groupthink
or you can watch TV commercials as if
they were aesthetic products to be
appreciated and analyzed: not much
of a choice, is it: let's go beyond
"either/or" and see if we can't just ignore
what offends our nostrils, and make
something out of our minds, out of our
minds in both senses: let's see
what happens when the imagination as
conceived by Wallace Stevens marries
the language as conceived by millions daily

January 20 ("The Gift Outright")

When Robert Frost recited "The Gift Outright"
in the gleaming cold noonday sun I was watching
there was no school I don't remember why
that afternoon we played touch football, my friends and I
on a sloping meadow in Fort Tryon Park
and life was going on elsewhere, life was going on downtown
in nightclubs that even then were going out of fashion
like the Stork Club or El Morocco and my friends and I
wanted to grow up and smoke cigarettes and drink highballs
and buy fur coats for our wives and take them to clubs
because that was life, and what we didn't realize
was that our afternoon in Fort Tryon Park
where we got into a fight with some Irish kids
was also life and even then was turning
into history with the Bay of Pigs and the Vienna summit
and Berlin and the missile crisis and the speech in Berlin
and the discotheques that put the nightclubs out of business
and Sam Giancana, the mob boss who would have
ordered a hit on Sinatra except he wanted
to hear him sing "Chicago" one more time

January 23 ("Ode to Modern Art")

Come on in and stay awhile
I'll photograph you emerging from the revolving door
like Frank O'Hara dating the muse of Fifty-third Street
Talking about the big Pollock show is better
than going to it on a dismal Saturday afternoon
when my luncheon partner is either the author or the subject
of *The Education of Henry Adams* at a hard-to-get-
a-table-at restaurant on Cornelia Street
just what is chaos theory anyway
I'm not sure but it helps explain *Autumn Rhythm*
the closest thing to chaos without crossing the border
I think you should write that book on Eakins and also the one
on nineteenth-century hats the higher the hat the sweller the toff
and together we will come up with Mondrian in the grid of Manhattan
Gerald Murphy's *Still Life with Wasp* and the best Caravaggio in the country
in Kansas City well it's been swell, see you in Cleveland April 23
The reason time goes faster as you grow older is that each day
is a tinier proportion of the totality of days in your life

February 11

She had the ugliest handwriting
and the prettiest green eyes
of any woman at the Museum
of Modern Art. She had
the loveliest legs and the smallest
apartment of any editor
at *Vogue*. She has the reddest
hair and the worst insomnia
of any actress on the Upper West Side.
She had the best mind and
the nastiest manners of any Swarthmore
graduate in the gym. She had
the meanest father and the leanest
mother and the crudest brother

and the lewdest sister and the most
money and the least compunction
of any divorcée in this room.
She had the sweetest voice.
She had the darkest moods.

February 21

If you were a monkey's uncle
and I were the monkey who wrote *Hamlet*
I'd explain why Wallace Stevens
is Keats on acid but then
we'd be back in the century of no return
and you'd turn into Lot's wife
and I'd follow the angels blindly
after washing their feet I'd hear
the explosions behind us and I'd picture
them a deep gash vermilion in the sky
red as a desert each poem a time
capsule meant to pop open on some
unspecified future day which will come
as surely as death comes as the end

February 28 ("Doubt")

I was a child he took me aside said
you've got a lot going for you
doubt, for one thing
you communicate doubt
as effectively as fickle freshmen
communicate illness
in their hospitable beds
and doubt is big this year
doubt is in, it's the condition
we're in, man,
and you mastered it

before you turned twenty-one
you had it mastered when
what you wanted to master
was nudity and Yale
you didn't know then how much
more fruitful is the world you mastered
of doubt
which you doubt

March 8

Every so often my father comes over
for a visit he hangs his overcoat and hat
on my hat rack I brief him on recent
developments and serve us coffee
he is surprised that I like to cook
once when he made an omelette
he flipped it in the air much to my delight
and it landed on the floor yes that
was the summer of 1952, he remembered
the high breakers and how fearless
I was running into the ocean anyway
the important thing is to see you doing
so well he said and took his coat and hat
and left before I remembered he was dead

March 30

Eighty-one degrees a record high for the day
which is not my birthday but will do until
the eleventh of June comes around and I know
what I want: a wide-brimmed Panama hat
with a tan hat band, a walk in the park
and to share a shower with the zaftig beauty
who lost her Bronx accent in Bronxville
and now wants me to give her back her virginity

so she slinks into my office and sits on the desk
and I, to describe her posture and pose,
will trade my Blake (the lineaments of a gratified
desire) for your Herrick (the liquefaction of
her clothes) though it isn't my birthday and
we're not still in college it's just a cup of coffee
and a joint the hottest thirtieth of March I've ever

April 24 ("Same Difference")

It occurred to me
today that there's
no difference between
"thank you" and "fuck you"
so from now on
whenever someone says
"thank you" to you
think of it as "fuck you"
OK but what about
the next time someone
says "fuck you" to you
does that mean "thank you"?
No, I'm afraid it doesn't work that way
(he smirked)
That also means "fuck you"
all roads lead to the Rome of "fuck you"
get it?
I do but you don't have to be so
fucking in-my-face about it
Well, fuck you
No, fuck you

May 26

In Rotterdam I'm
going to speak about

the state of poetry
on a panel with a Pole
and a Turk. It's worth
being alive to utter
that sentence. A
German from Fürth,
my father's home town
and Henry Kissinger's,
will preside. His name
is Joachim Sartorius,
which sounds like a
pseudonym Kierkegaard
might use to condemn
the habits of his age
and ours when nothing
ever happens but the
publicity is immediate
and the town meeting
ends with the people
convinced they have
rebelled so now they
can go home quietly
having spent a most
pleasant evening

June 4

I said OK Joe what makes
this flower beautiful
what makes the flower
a flower he answered
right again as we walked
down Valentine Place past
the students and the nursing
home down the cobblestone
street leading to the bridge
above Six Mile Creek where

myrtle grows wild I wonder
why Milton said "ye myrtles
brown" when they're green with
little purple buds in May

July 20

When I think of all the Annes
in my life they're all you almost
you're the Irish girl with the blonde
corkscrew curls in Cincinnati but
you're also Anne of the thousand
days and poems my mother's
name is Anne the heroine of my
novel of the twentieth century
which begins in Vienna moves
to London with Freud and sneaks into
New York during the "phony war"
in 1939 Anne is the name of the first girl
I loved and it's always spelled with an *e*
I lost my virginity to a Brandeis girl
named Anne and a Sarah Lawrence girl
named Anne lost hers to me I'm a big
fan of Anne and will always be

August 16 ("Rap")

I'm still here (Ithaca)
the students are back
they drive up next door
in a Mercedes sports car
the color of a school bus
hideous, with rap music
to announce their arrival they
leave the car running, the keys inside,
the music on while they go inside the house

I walk over remove the keys
toss them in the bushes walk away
unobserved & think of Ashbery's line
there's only one thing worse than rap music:
French rap music

August 25 ("Commencement")

They're calling old people seniors
short for senior citizens but it's as though
they're still in college and can look forward
to graduate school at Purgatory State
or the University of the Damned and
I can see this poem is intent on being Catholic
though it started out agnostic
Maybe that's because I was talking
to Ed Webster on the phone tonight
and he described himself as an agnostic
who got a job teaching at a Catholic school
in the South Bronx or maybe because I was reading
the classifieds in the *Daily News* today
and several greeted dead ones in heaven
in any case I like seniors maybe the rest of us
are juniors and sophomores and we still have
the junior prom and all that romantic angst
to go through before we reach the holy land

September 5

Latrell Sprewell is the Marlon Brando
of the Knicks and the definition
of schadenfreude is my hollow laugh
when I tell you how Frank Kermode
lost two-thirds of his library
to the men he thought were movers
who were actually garbagemen

and the one-third of his library
spared was literary theory
which he used to be tolerant of
in a laissez-faire spirit but
has grown to detest now that
it no longer matters what
he thinks and you say Columbia
paid him not to teach the way
the government pays farmers not
to farm their land and now I know
how I want to spend this lazy day
the Sunday of Labor Day weekend
with a pot of coffee in my pajamas
all morning and you on the phone

September 7

Not a day without a notation
each woman loved because of
a woman she reminded me of
is that true no it's a theory
I'm going to kiss those lying lips
of yours for oh love's bow
shoots buck and doe and the impulse
to theorize is irresistible in
the evening sun we came as close
to having sex as two people could
without having sex in the nude swimming
capital of upstate New York & though
I've never seen her since I feel about
that girl as did Everett Sloane about
the girl he saw on the ferry
in his memory when he was suffering
from old age, the disease whose cure
is worse than the ailment, in *Citizen Kane*

October 2

While I wondered about the relation
of fraud to Freud and both to joy
my Wellesley girlfriend, a dyslexic
classics major, wanted to discuss
the "myth of syphilis" meanwhile
Jim Cummins confesses he lives in
"a witness protection program called
Ohio" and the critics sit in judgment
of John Keats and what he meant
by melancholy in his ode "I think
Keats is saying 'deal with it'" one says
not the one who calls him John Maynard
Keats but you can't have everything
("bucks, tenure") all you can count on
is unremitting indifference
broken up by patches of hostility

October 11

The language is full of sad words
but the saddest of these is Dad
the contest between fathers and sons
is an unequal one like the proportion
of combat to uneasy nonaggression
in *War and Peace* or World War II
still the weekend has to be counted
a success with two meals cooked by Dad
duck in Chinatown last night and a bacon-
burger for breakfast this morning at Aggie's
the Mets won, *The Blair Witch Project*
was spooky as advertised and there were
surprises too I think I like those the most
and now for a "serene" (his word) moment
in Joe's honor in Washington Square Park
awful noise of boom boxes I don't hear them

the sky like a body of water blue
with a single sail and light wind

November 14 ("A Quick One Before I Go")

There comes a time in every man's life
when he thinks: I have never had a single
original thought in my life
including this one & therefore I shall
eliminate all ideas from my poems
which shall consist of cats, rice, rain
baseball cards, fire escapes, hanging plants
redbrick houses where I shall give up booze
and organized religion even if it means
despair is a logical possibility that can't
be disproved I shall concentrate on the five
senses and what they half perceive and half
create, the green street signs with white
letters on them the body next to mine
asleep while I think these thoughts
that I want to eliminate like nostalgia
O was there ever a man who felt as I do
like a pronoun out of step with all the other
floating signifiers no things but in words
an orange T-shirt a lime green awning

November 22

Poetry is
posing a
question to
the universe
and getting
no for
an answer
or getting

no answer
I'm not
sure which

December 8

Fathers die twice
a year in Judaism
my father died today
twenty-eight years ago
in the secular calendar
and on 20 Kislev (November
29 this year) in the Hebrew
so I mourn on both dates
with a candle after many
ghostly reappearances
in Elsinore my home for
all the big speeches and
years I thought Freud's
Hamlet was the true one and
could be played by me in my
daily life while at night I moon-
lighted as Samuel Taylor Coleridge

December 30

There are two scenarios
in one the market crashes
our hero loses some money
not all being a conservative
sort with a wife whose
charms were wasted on him
in the other the market crashes
and he loses most of his money
and goes off to fight the Trojan
War in either case there's

only one constant and that's
Heisenberg's Uncertainty
Principle the old reliable it hadn't
failed him yet though everything
else was changing well it was better
after all to be the author of the epic
than any of the characters even
the heroes Hector saying goodbye
to Andromache holding their baby

from *The Daily Mirror:*

A Journal in Poetry (2000)

January 1

Some people confuse inspiration with lightning
not me I know it comes from the lungs and air
you breathe it in you breathe it out it circulates
it's the breath of my being the wind across the face
of the waters yes but it's also something that comes
at my command like a turkey club sandwich
with a cup of split pea soup or like tones
from Benny Goodman's clarinet my clarinet
the language that never fails to respond
some people think you need to be pure of heart
not true it comes to the pure and impure alike
the patient and impatient the lovers the onanists
and the virgins you just need to be able to listen
and talk at the same time and you'll hear it like
the long-delayed revelation at the end of the novel
which turns out to be something simple a traumatic
moment that fascinated us more when it was only
a fragment an old song a strange noise a mistake
in hearing a phone that wouldn't stop ringing

January 5

Every time I hear
a new word I see
a new color, Joe
said in the cab. For
example, I said.
For example, he

said, the word
"example" is yellow,
brown, olive & a
little white mashed
together. And each
letter of the alphabet
has an age, a sex, &
a personality. H, for
example, is a lavender
girl, fourteen, a friend
of the number 4, who
is also a girl and also
lavender. And I? I
asked. I, he said,
is a genius, white.

January 14

Let's play Word Golf you go from
"love" to "hate" in fourteen lines
or from "kiss" to "fuck" one letter
at a time, like going from soft
to soot to loot to loft to lift
to life, that's my idea but Anne
Winters wants us to write a poem
ending with the line "and I die
of thirst at the fountain's rim"
so of course everyone does both
the snow like sea foam
surrounding a marooned sailor
stretches out before me, and how easy
it is for that mariner to swim
to shore a desert island where
he explores every inch on his belly
looking for water and dies
of thirst at the fountain's rim

January 24

I was about to be mugged by a man
with a chain so angry he growled
at the Lincoln Center subway station
when out of nowhere appeared a tall
chubby-faced Hasidic Jew with *peyot*
and a black hat a black coat white shirt
with prayer shawl fringes showing
we walked together out of the station
and when we got outside and shook hands
I noticed he was blind. Goodbye,
I said, as giddy as a man waking
from an anesthetic in the recovery room,
happy, with a hard-on. The cabs were
on strike on Broadway so beautiful
a necklace of yellow beads
I breathed in the fumes impossibly happy

January 26

Freedom is wonderful
You can choose not to know
the names of actors and blues bands
or the teams playing in the Super Bowl
You can go to bed instead
of going to the movies
and if you're lucky the person
next to you will be you
of the curly locks what a coincidence
how sweet to think of all the routes
we have taken to arrive at this moment
and I wonder whether we were ever
in the same place at the same time
before we knew each other
and now good morrow to our waking souls
I am going to commit your scent to memory

and when you aren't here you'll still be here
and the person kissing you will be me

February 6

Intense, volatile, temperamental,
will not win amiability award or be
elected president of temple or club,
anxious to the point of taking action
in the form of needless phone calls
and letters to the editor, loses temper
on phone with staff underlings
and their bosses who call up
five minutes later to complain,
and thus is spent another glorious
morning on the job, stressed out,
pissed off, but still able to muster up
the old magic to explain why
one of the greatest sentences
of the twentieth century is,
"My mother was a saint"

March 4

There's a potion I take
every day it contains echinacea,
osha, garlic, goldenseal,
ginger, chaparral, horse-
radish, usnea, cayenne,
and vodka I bought it in
Ithaca a place called Oasis
the bearded guy said his
wife made the stuff you
take it three weeks then
go off it and chew three
juniper berries every day

for a week I love Ithaca
when I'm not there in the
winter and my lilac bushes
are waiting for May
when I will come back
to admire them in full bloom

March 11

What common object
can be dialed on the phone
using only the numbers two and four?
hint: it is seven letters long
is it important like the night
I was asked my opinion of the painter
Jeff Koons and I pointed out
his name spelled backwards was Snook
and today with Nat Cole's silk voice
in my ear as I drive from Joe's school
where Andrea, the principal, tells me
she's taking a class in advanced astrology
she's a Libra but her moon in Scorpio
keeps her from being a wishy-washy type
I love Ithaca on mornings like this one
nothing like the sound of dripping water
that once was snow to cheer one up
and after watching *The Wild Bunch* last night
Joe said I'm going to write a sequel
to my philosophy of life and call it
Brilliant Carnage

March 15

Wisdom has the logic
of a haiku not a syllogism
the difference is spring

the light lasting longer
in March the month of mud
when hungry, eat
when angry, cool off
if a woman named Karen
comes to check your gas meter
do not jump her everyone's
in the mood I haven't seen a crocus
or a rosebud but "It Might as Well
Be Spring" on the radio
Archie phones and says
he's high on Coke which
in our private code means
he's bullish on Coca-Cola stock
which has already doubled and split
but just wait till they get to China

March 24

I remember England when sleep was
like a wrestling match with the sea
I dreamed my father had died and
when he did I dreamed he was alive
and woke up battered on the rocks
in any case twenty-five years ago
but today despite my nightmare of
an empty auditorium when I mount
the podium, I wake to let sleep
swallow me again, care-charmer sleep
with a comet glowing in the dark,
and a warm shower to wash the dust
out of my eyes, and the day begins
with "Do Nothing till You Hear from Me"
jazz is the art of phrasing as
poetry is the art of timing what we
want from both is refreshment
we can never get enough of

let day be time enough to mourn
the shipwreck of my sea-tossed youth
I will listen to songs unlimited
in the deep dark chambers of sleep

March 30

In *The Best Years of Our Lives*
the frank and friendly smile
of Dana Andrews who couldn't get
a job despite his Distinguished
Flying Cross he was my idea
of what a grown-up man should
look like wearing a tie with
his bomber jacket, a soda jerk
in a drugstore, and a double-
breasted suit to his pal's wedding
one of the fallen angels
of the air force why is it when
I go to the movies today I
rarely believe the male lead
is a grown-up in the old-fashioned
sense of fathers who went to work
downtown every morning is it
because I'm one of them now
when I wanted to be Dana Andrews

April 2

What I like about reading in the dark is
you can't see what you're reading
and must imagine verses equal to your longing
and then Keats shows up with "La Belle Dame
Sans Merci" and Yeats wonders whether
"you" will ever be loved for yourself alone
and not your yellow hair

when I was a Columbia freshman
we had to compare those two poems
I wish I were asked to do that today
for I have finally figured it out
but at the time all I could think to say
was that both women, the one whose eyes
were shut with kisses four
and the one with the yellow hair,
were the same woman, and I knew her

April 3

I like movies like dreams that
jumble the order of events
there is no past in a dream
everything is happening now
so you can be married and
divorced and still be the boy
whose father took him to see
*How to Succeed in Business
Without Really Trying* with
Michele Lee as Rosemary in 1965
two years later I was reviewing
plays for the Columbia *Spectator*
it's fun to write about something
you know nothing about like
*Rosencrantz and Guildenstern
Are Dead* I forget what was wrong
with it but something was that's
what criticism is "all about"
plus a few remarks about parody,
chance, and the absurd, just as
poetry is "all about" time which
equals love times death squared

April 6

She's a high-maintenance doll
at two in the morning she starts
talking the pauses between your
answers grow longer she says
"you're not listening" you repeat
what she said she says "that's
just a trick you weren't really
listening" and before you know it
you're snoring in her ear a version
of "I Wished on the Moon" by Billie
Holiday and the moon slips under
the sea chased by a whippet
who is licking your neck ah fidelity
to wake up and she's still there
there is something to be said
in favor of five hours of sleep
on this Saturday when the clocks
spring forward and you spring into
action because she wants her coffee
and no one else is in on the secret

April 9

I woke up not in Paris
that's the first thing that went wrong
after the pleasure of a week
of speaking French badly
also the smoke detector went off
when I made coffee,
and my telephone lacks a dial tone
so I know I'm back in the greatest city
with my incomparable view of garbage
in the alley out the window with sun
a bright white on red brick turning yellow
and just enough blue to imply a sky

high enough and far enough away
to stand for all that's mind (mine)

April 15

What a sweet guy I am
when one of my enemies dies
I don't Xerox the obit and mail it
to the others saying "Let
this be a lesson to you," no
I'm more likely to recall
the person's virtues to which I
was blind until the news of mortality
opened my mind as you would
open a vial of Tylenol noticing
it spells "lonely" backwards with
only the initial T added, signifying
taxes no doubt, and now my headache
has gone the way of leaves in fall
am I happy I certainly am
as you would be, my friend, if
the Queen of Sheba returned your calls
as she does mine

April 26

When my father
said *mein Fehler*
I thought it meant
"I'm a failure"
which was my error
which is what
mein Fehler means
in German which
is what my parents
spoke at home

April 27 or 28

As Hamlet would have said
if he had lived through
the Russian Revolution and
his author had written in Russian,
"To live a life is not to cross
a field." I think I see what he
means, or would have meant,
by that line so hard to translate,
yet I wouldn't underestimate
the difficulty of crossing a field,
a snow-covered expanse, say,
wide as the Steppes, that no
footprints have defaced, so that,
staring at it, you feel like
a writer facing a blank page,
and the trees may be full of rifles,
and the whole reason for crossing
the field escapes you now that
you have reached its edge,
and the rumor of a castle
on a high hill in the distance
is almost certain to turn out false.

April 29

God bless Wellbutrin
I see the market's down
a hundred and forty points
but I don't care I know
it will go up again tomorrow
thanks to the Dead Cat Bounce
as "the Street" terms it
still I refuse to invest in El Niño
by buying soybean futures
on the Chicago Options Exchange

I'd rather phone Joe who answers,
"You have reached WJOE,
all Joe Lehman, all the time,"
as for the guy who reviewed Jim
Tate's book and called it "almost
Victorian in its piety," I got news
for you, buddy, not even the Victorians
were Victorian in their piety have you
ever read "In Memoriam" or "Dover Beach"
well, have you, punk?

May 2

Someday I'd like to go
to Atlantic City with you
not to gamble (just being
there with you is enough
of a gamble) but to ride
the high white breakers
have a Manhattan and listen
to a baritone saxophone
play a tune called "Salsa
Eyes" with you beside me
on a banquette but why
stop there let's go to
Paris in November when
it's raining and we read
the *Tribune* at La Rotonde
our hotel room has a big
bathtub I knew you'd like
that and we can be a couple
of unknown Americans what
are we waiting for let's go

May 6

The brain has chambers
on different floors
a warren of offices
upstairs a library
a wine cellar below
but the soul is simple
like a mother who
packs your lunchbox
and you walk home
wearing the raincoat
she made you take
though it is sunny
and mild my mother
when I was four was
talking to another
mother and I strayed off
and went to the park
and found someone to
walk me home where I sat
on a car waiting for
her to come back she was
frantic but when she saw
me she laughed the soul
is a hungry boy eating
her soup in the kitchen

May 10

The best way to learn a foreign language
is to go to the place and rent a car
with a little Berlitz phrase book
In every language there's one sentence
the tourist must learn
In Italian it's Excuse me where's the church
of Santa Maria della Vittoria

155

In French it's Do you have any brake fluid?
In German it's What did I do wrong?
In English it's I'm sorry to have to tell you
that Gerry Freund died
and there's nothing you can do about it
you can't phone him up to say
you'll miss him

July 13

I'm going to miss you, Robert Mitchum,
as I make my rounds in lower Manhattan
checking the progress of Joe DiMaggio's
56-game hitting streak the way you did
in *Farewell, My Lovely*. Next to Bogart
you were the best Philip Marlowe. Smart,
too. Getting arrested for marijuana use the
year I was born was a shrewd career move.
Sleepless by instinct, you looked like
a car mechanic and were a fighter whose best
moment came when he got off the canvas
and took another punch. You lost every fight
with the woman in the houseboat who sang
"There's a fire down below in my heart."
She came out of the past and now at last
you've joined her in some South American
beach where escaped convicts dream
of going, and I'm walking on Sixth Avenue
with your groggy voice in my mind
daring the world to surprise you.

July 15

Just as a company's closing stock price today
reflects expert estimates of its future earnings,
so, in the economy of the psyche,

anxiety is the fear of future unhappiness,
and as desire always exceeds its fulfillment
disappointment is inevitable that's my theory
of surplus desire as for insomnia
it's the organism's natural defense
against the fear of its extinction
animals don't sleep when they're afraid
and neither should we
still a defense of anxiety may be mounted
on the grounds that you can convert it
to adrenaline as actors do on opening night
or parachutists who know fear is the greatest high

October 11

Of cities I know New York
wins the paranoia award
the place you'd least like
to be stuck between floors
on a temperamental elevator
on 14th Street or ride on
the N train when the
conductor's face is missing
that must be why we like it
we who like to think we
thrive on risk on the other
hand the discrepancy
between the cold air
outside and the overheated
flat is without parallel and
completely without justification

November 10

The bridges that make Manhattan an island
and Brooklyn part of another island

I sing
as Joe and I cross the Williamsburg Bridge
on the way back from our tour of the Brooklyn Brewery
where Joe asks whether it's true that atoms must be split
to make beer no not atoms but molecules do
and hops are added in the last five minutes for their aroma
and to counteract with bitterness the excess sugar
we sample the brews Joe favors the wheat beer I the Belgian ale
and afterwards we are walking down Seventh Avenue
and Joe says he loves the city because
he has to walk fast to keep up with his old man,
and the funny thing is the same is true for me

November 13

for Mark Stevens

I want your opinion
of my manuscript
my friend because
you know Art
and I know Art Linkletter
but you have a deadline
to meet while I have a date
with a certain great novelist
in my apartment
whose idea of heaven is the men's room
of Grand Central Station
and hell a prison in a posh suburb
with a swimming pool where
you can feel like a fly in a highball
you read one sentence and you know
the number of martinis
that went through that
system is not to be
counted on an ordinary abacus

November 17

Who wants a mass-market audience
I just want a mass-market bankbook
with a little privacy and enough energy
for all the days of the year
as they come, stay awhile, and leave
with Bartók's *Pieces for Orchestra*
on the radio as the windows darken
just before evening arrives
I want this moment, no other will do,
to conceive of great debates between
the self and the soul
battling it out in verse
the self fluent as a sestina
the soul reduced to seventeen syllables
the self a cosmos or a public frog
the soul a self-described nobody
the self getting in the last word
the soul content with a laugh

November 19

for Beth Ann Fennelly

Do I still like to think
of myself in the third
person? I do, I mean,
he does. He liked, too,
to read the paper on
the couch with a cup
of coffee in his robe
daydreaming of a girl
he hadn't met who
liked doing a pirouette
in an ankle-length
silvery gray skirt

that flares in a full
circle when she does so.
Not that she planned
to do so on stage, but
it was nice to know
she could. She thought
of herself as a fair warrior
on the strand hearing
the warring voices
of the sea, and he was
her demon lover, who
liked sitting around
dreaming of the things
he liked, like the girl
who shoplifted lipstick
because she liked
the sound of its name.

November 23

Went to *The Waste Land* last night
Fiona Shaw's one-woman show
in a derelict theater
on West 42nd Street it was
the first poem of the 20th century
in which bad sex is a metaphor
for the failure of civilization
which is searching for a place
by a placid lake where it can have
a nervous breakdown in peace and quiet
the first poem of the 20th century
to resemble a crossword puzzle
the clues in the form of fragments
phantom quotations and the image
of Eliot in a bedroom with a monastic bed
and a single unadorned lightbulb
in the ceiling he was the straightest-

looking poet of the 20th century
with a superb cover, a banker's
three-piece suit, but he was as bonkers
as the rest of us, with rats and bones
and dry rocks rattling around his brain
and a drowned sailor's swollen eyeballs

November 26

I used to think other people's
lives were more real than mine.
Journalists covering a war could
talk about truth and commitment
in an open-air jeep, smoking.
Movie stars could run for Congress
on a rock-and-roll platform
and I could make fun of them but
secretly I envied the woman next door
who went to her office every day
where she "pushed papers and crunched
numbers," she told me, without
explaining what that meant. But
she felt part of the great extravaganza,
Thanksgiving, Christmas, the works—
in love on New Year's Eve,
by Valentine's Day brokenhearted—
while I stayed in my apartment
searching for words to describe
feelings that had already departed.

December 12

There's an old French saying,
"the whole of a man's mystery
rests in his hat," and if you
translate it into American

you get Sinatra smoking
and singing "Memories of
You," "I Thought About You,"
"You Make Me Feel So Young,"
and "You Brought a New
Kind of Love to Me," all
from the same 1956 session,
I love that voice and have since
the summer I was eight and
my friend Ann and I sang "Love
and Marriage" on Talent Night
at the bungalow colony when I'm
down there's nothing like you,
birthday boy, singing "All of Me"
to lift me up and when I'm in love
I jump out of bed in the morning
singing "It All Depends on You" and
your voice comes out of my mouth

December 14

This bed thy center is, these walls, thy sphere,
The tarnished, gaudy, wonderful old work
Of hand, of foot, of lip, of eye, of brow,
That never touch with inarticulate pang
Those dying generations—at their song.
The One remains, the many change and pass
The expiring swan, and as he sings he dies.
The earth, the stars, the light, the day, the skies,
A white-haired shadow roaming like a dream
Limitless out of the dusk, out of the cedars and pines,
Think not of them, thou hast thy music too—
Sin and her shadow Death, and Misery,
If but some vengeful god would call to me,
Because I could not stop for Death,
Not to return. Earth's the right place for love.
My playmate, when we both were clothed alike,

Should I, after tea and cakes and ices,
Suffer my genial spirits to decay
Upon the bridal day, which is not long?
I thought that love would last forever; I was wrong.

December 17

In the great fox versus hedgehog debate
that Isaiah Berlin sponsored—
the hedgehog who does one
thing versus the fox who does many—
I come down firmly on the side of the fox,
and today's manuscripts, letters, faxes,
e-mails, and succession of phone calls
overlapping each other like a version
of serial monogamy proves it: any day
beginning with a phone call from John
Ashbery is a good one and then there was
lunch with Glen at Bruxelles, chapters
of my book to photocopy, a new title
for these poems *(The Daily Mirror*—
like it?), and why am I so exhilarated?
as if the blood in my veins ran as fast
and recklessly as the traffic down Fifth
and the lights in the top story windows
shine in rooms where I am writing

December 29

I spent a month writing love poems
to women I didn't know (see May 7),
women I had met for a whole half
hour (August 18), fictional characters,
composite dream-drenched figures,
and all for the pleasure of being
a French poet in prewar Paris, having

a Gauloise and an espresso on the run,
I had vast metaphors to make,
no sooner did I have an idea than
I would witness its fulfillment,
a tower or a bridge, and head on
to the next project and of course you
were there with me the whole time
though unnamed in the rain as if
nothing could be more romantic
than a shared umbrella

from *Valentine Place* (1996)

Wedding Song

Poetry is a criticism of life
As a jailbreak is a criticism of prison.
I now pronounce you man and wife.

The pencil has no chance against the knife,
You can't compete with television.
Poetry used to be a criticism of life.

Because you play together like a drum and fife
On the Fourth of July, your favorite season,
I now pronounce you man and wife.

The sonnets resisted, though they were rife
With clues subjected to a critic's misprision:
Poetry may not be a criticism of life.

In a field full of purple loosestrife,
Does happiness require a reason?
I now pronounce you man and wife.

The fruits of peace, to be peeled with a knife,
Await your teeth. It's your decision.
Is poetry a criticism of life?
I now pronounce you man and wife.

Breeze Marine

La chair est triste, hélas! et j'ai lu tous les livres.
—Mallarmé, "Brise Marine"

The impeccable old man, who chaired the committee,
Reported a vague but pervasive sadness
In the land, causing the people who lived by the sea
To stare at the sea for hours, with their backs to the land,
Inhaling deeply, dreaming of platters of oysters and clams.
The boy nodded. He knew that patriotism was just
A craving for food loved as a boy in Rockaway Beach.

The boy was disappointed with the sins of the flesh,
The sadness after sex.
Not guilt, though sometimes that, too, entered into it,
But a sort of dazed surprise to find where lust had led him.

The man said:
"O what a magnificent invention was the id
Freud fashioned out of the dreams and errors
Of turn-of-the-century neurotics in Vienna,
The city where Hitler grew up, wanting to become a painter."

"But that does not explain the sadness, or invalidate it,"
The boy replied.

The man looked at the boy and said:
"Although you may read many books, so many
You imagine you have read them all,
There will always be one more on the shelf above your bed
You will not be able to finish before falling asleep.
Remember: to escape into a novel about French decadence
Is as good as escaping via a seaworthy vessel
Headed for mutiny in the South Seas.
If there's anything the nineteenth century taught us, it's that."

The boy shelved the novel, turned around,
And walked away without a sound.

This is what he thought:

"Evil tears. Sad flesh. Paper void.
The moment of grace was when
The misfit held a gun to the old woman's temple.
In this place, prayer is the howl of a dog,
The rabbi strangled with his own prayer shawl.
The last words he heard were, 'Kill the Jew.'
That was how he knew that God was watching.

"I will never forget that moment.
The wailing was terrible, the sirens unbearable.

"The hero turns around at this point
As the true dimensions of the catastrophe dawn on him
At last. There is a pink glow in the distance,
Faint; a whiff of salt in his nostrils. He sees
Handkerchiefs waved by ladies in white dresses.
He hears the horns of departure. Nothing can stop him now!"

Picking up the pen he sat for a moment
Daunted by the whiteness of the page. It was like
Snow on college lawns before footprints deface it.

Those footprints were going to be his,
Even now he could picture the path, leading to the past,
A particular June morning, a tryst in Hellas,
White waves, cries of gulls. The bunch of grapes.
An instant, and it was gone. The place was
The place he'd dreamed about in his dreams of escape.

Boy with Red Hair

1.

The boy was shy. He was quietly bored in the dark house but too nice
     to say so.

One afternoon at three thirty the mother didn't show up and the boy
     had to take a taxi from school to house. He was furious with
     her. "He was so angry he reminded me of you," the mother
     told her ex-husband.

I guess I inherit my absent-mindedness from her, said the boy.
He was old-fashioned, with freckles and red hair,
and when they drove through a toll booth
the man at the toll booth would say, "Hi, Red."

The boy and his grandfather had several things in common.
Both were soft-spoken, sincere hypochondriacs.
Their favorite fruits were strawberries in summer
and pears in fall.

A parrot alighted on the boy's shoulder.
See, the cage's door was wide open the whole time.
Later, the boy made eye contact
with a butterfly settling on his shoe.

The boy was slow in the bathroom, thinking
while brushing his teeth.

What was he thinking about?
"Did you know Jack Nicholson played a killer
in *Cry Baby Killer*, his first movie?"

Hours later he couldn't reconstruct the thought processes that had led
to this moment.

2.

The boy put his yellow-and-brown-checked pajama bottoms
around his head and became Invulnerable Man.
Swinging himself around,
he knocked down a vase, which crashed.
And then he got quiet, very quiet.

The boy had a respect for silence.
He didn't say one word more than was strictly necessary.
On the phone he would say *uh-huh* and *yes* and little else.

He liked long car trips. His father asked,
What would you paint—the clouds
or the trees—if you were a painter?
The boy thought for what seemed like a long time.
He thought it would be difficult to paint the clouds.
Ladders weren't long enough.

3.

That night he slept in the Château d'If.

"Do not underestimate me," said the German commandant.
"From this prison there is no escape."
The boy had heard these words before. He knew what came next.
The commandant needed to make an example of somebody.
He would pick a prisoner at random and have him hanged.
This would frighten the others,

and the hunger strike would be over.
In prison there was plenty of time to imagine the scene.

In prison there was time to waste, wondering why he was there,
making appeals, pleading for a hearing,
when he should have been playing on the porch
listening to the birds singing
or digging a tunnel from his bed
to the mad priest's cell, substituting
his body for the dead man's in the shroud
after memorizing the map of his secret treasure,
ready to return to life, to swim all the way
to Paris if necessary, a nobleman in a cape,
ready to exact his revenge.

Flashback

The lonely boy in the blue snowsuit playing
With the dog that didn't exist
In the yard of the house that hadn't yet been built
Was the older brother I never had, and he was
Carving a snow palace guarded by soldiers and stone lions
Where violins played waltzes from the Vienna woods
While in the big bay window in the living room
You could see the mouths of his parents moving
And though you couldn't hear the words
You knew a divorce was in the cards, and then you see
A close-up of the mother's face and suddenly
You can tell what she will look like in twenty years
And what she looked like twenty years ago.
The boy vanishes. It continues to snow.

Who She Was

She loved jumping on the trampoline.
Her nickname was Monkey.
She slipped her tongue in his mouth when they kissed.

She had a job in publishing. It was what
she most wanted after she got out of Vassar. The first
manuscript she acquired was *The Heidegger Cookbook*,
so you can imagine how her career took off from there.

She started liking sex soon after her husband left her.
He came back weekends and complied
with her bedtime wishes. A lawyer.
What did you expect? A Peace Corps
volunteer who went on to become
the editor of *Envy: The Magazine for You?*

Where did her anger come from? He wasn't sure
but it was how he knew she loved him.

It was heartbreaking to learn that they
had both married other people. "What is the most
heartbreaking thing you can think of?"
he asked. Her list included the dawn,
Vassar graduation, and the city
of Paris, which she described in vivid prose
before she set foot in France. It was

the one infallible rule she used
to write her acclaimed series of travel guidebooks.

He realized why he married her:
so he wouldn't have to think about her,
or about sex, or about other women: the hours
they consumed like crossword puzzles
and chocolate-covered cherries.

She said the most obvious things
but she said them well.

She tried to impress people but kept blundering
as when she attributed the phrase "Make It New"
to William Carlos Williams.

She had the soul of a stranger.
There were things that she loved besides herself—
flowers, poems.

She was obsessed with the difficulty
of finding good nectarines in New York City.
They cost an arm and a leg and were mealy.

She said something critical
He flew off the handle
She asked, "Are you saying it's over?"
He said Fuck you
She said Fuck you and told him to leave
All right, he said, I'm leaving
if that's the way you want it
and if you want to know
where I am, I'm in Palm Springs
fucking Lana Turner
as Frank Sinatra put it to Ava Gardner
who was in her bathtub at the time
it was 1952

She got so depressed she stayed in her room
all day. At least that way she would stay
out of trouble. Her job kept her sedentary.
The only exercise she got was fixing a sandwich
and writing dialogue for a man and a woman
while one is packing a suitcase: "What are you
doing?" "What does it look like I'm doing?"

It rained all day, converting a September morning
into a November afternoon. The speed
of thinking was faster than the speed of light.
"How's your ex-wife?"
"She's divorced, too," he replied.
"That's what we have in common."

He had the odd habit of smiling when he was tense.
This made him a lousy poker player but won her sympathy.
She liked his bohemian life. Or didn't really
but said she did. The joy went out of his eyes
but the smile stayed on his face
having nowhere else to go. God's image
was shaving in the mirror, feeling like hell,
missing her, wondering who she was.

The World Trade Center

I never liked the World Trade Center.
When it went up I talked it down
as did many other New Yorkers.
The twin towers were ugly monoliths
that lacked the details the ornament the character
of the Empire State Building and especially
the Chrysler Building, everyone's favorite,
with its scalloped top, so noble.
The World Trade Center was an example of what was wrong
with American architecture,
and it stayed that way for twenty-five years
until that Friday afternoon in February
when the bomb went off and the buildings became
a great symbol of America, like the Statue
of Liberty at the end of Hitchcock's *Saboteur*.
My whole attitude toward the World Trade Center
changed overnight. I began to like the way
it comes into view as you reach Sixth Avenue
from any side street, the way the tops
of the towers dissolve into white skies
in the east when you cross the Hudson
into the city across the George Washington Bridge.

(1993)

Sexism

The happiest moment in a woman's life
Is when she hears the turn of her lover's key
In the lock, and pretends to be asleep
When he enters the room, trying to be
Quiet but clumsy, bumping into things,
And she can smell the liquor on his breath
But forgives him because she has him back
And doesn't have to sleep alone.

The happiest moment in a man's life
Is when he climbs out of bed
With a woman, after an hour's sleep,
After making love, and pulls on
His trousers, and walks outside,
And pees in the bushes, and sees
The high August sky full of stars
And gets in his car and drives home.

from "Valentine Place"

First Lines

Mother was born today. I traveled back to watch her
In the school play, crying because her mother wasn't there.
There was always a crisis in the tailor shop in Vienna.
Father smoked cigars. What he liked about his life was
The chance to do the same thing twice—to lose the lady
A second time, flee from Europe, and live in a grand hotel,
Looking sharp in a tuxedo among the gambling tables.
If childhood is a foreign country, his had armed guards
At the barbed-wire border. "Don't you remember me,"
The lady asked plaintively. He shook his head no, grinning
Like a soldier before combat, "But I'm willing to learn."
Sometimes the memory of her face was all that kept him going.
He had to see her again. It didn't matter where or when.
They would go to Coney Island, eat hot dogs, be American.
America was young then, naïve, brash, confident.
The immigrants were pouring in: new blood, old guts.
And when the market crashed, and banks started failing,
My old man gave me a piece of advice that I've never
Forgotten, though I never did manage to follow it.
Get the money. Cut your losses. Always look your partner
In the eye, except when kissing her warm red lips,
Drunk on her aroma, surprised to be alive.

Second Thoughts

What a life: hospitals and airports, clocks in corridors,
Mother asleep in the next room, and Dad waking up to piss,
Knocking over the glass of water and the vial of pills
On the night table. It took him all these years
To learn that America hated eggheads and queers,
And death was everywhere, a foreign language
Spoken by everybody but him: the old people obsessed
With their money, and the predatory brokers
In their strip mall offices, making steeples
Out of their hands. America was New York, but New York
Was moving South, going fast, reaching Miami in 1979,
The year marijuana use reached an all-time high
In high schools; he read about it in the national edition
Of today's *Times*. Today he was with the two people
He loved best in all the world, and the level
Of hysteria, always high, was rising in the living room.
Why was it so hard to make them happy? The party
Was over twelve years ago, yet only now did he realize it
Driving with his friend from Coral Gables
In her big red Buick, with Frank Sinatra on the tape deck
And the Biltmore Hotel out the window. These palm trees
Made him happy. They were Miami when life was real.

Sixth Sense

Something told him she was near. In the same room,
Even. Wearing the blue polka-dot dress he'd given her,
With the pearl choker and the sapphire earrings,
Holding a Kir Royale. He looked at her left hand.
No ring. And knew he had to get out of there
Fast, before one of them did something irrevocable,
Like the time she slapped his face in the bus
And he wasn't sure why, or the day they stood
In front of the dress-shop window, and when

She said she liked the yellow kimono he went
And bought it on the spot. What an amazing day
That was. Everyone he met that day was someone
He had known before, a decade ago or more,
And the statue of Alice the gigantic girl
In Central Park turned out to be his sister
When they were small. Mama was in the kitchen
Waiting for the phone to ring, and Daddy was still
On the road, checking the rearview mirror
In the old green Chevrolet, when the hurricane hit.
One of the other men drowned that night, but Daddy
Came back safely, with gifts for all the kids
If they agreed to go to sleep and dream of him.

Tenth Commandment

The woman said yes she would go to Australia with him
Unless he heard wrong and she said Argentina
Where they could learn the tango and pursue the widows
Of Nazi war criminals unrepentant to the end.
But no, she said Australia. She'd been born in New Zealand.
In the candy store across from the elementary school,
They planned their tryst. She said Australia, which meant
She was willing to go to bed with him, and this
Was before her husband's coronary
At a time when a woman didn't take off her underpants
If she didn't like you. She said Australia,
And he saw last summer's seashell collection
In a plastic bag on a shelf in the mudroom
With last summer's sand. The cycle of sexual captivity
Beginning in romance and ending in adultery
Was now in the late middle phases, the way America
Had gone from barbarism to amnesia without
A period of high decadence, which meant something,
But what? A raft on the rapids? The violinist
At the gate? Oh, absolute is the law of biology.
For the pornography seminar, what should she wear?

Eleventh Hour

The bloom was off the economic recovery.
"I just want to know one thing," she said.
What was that one thing? He'll never know,
Because at just that moment he heard the sound
Of broken glass in the bathroom, and when he got there,
It was dark. His hand went to the wall
But the switch wasn't where it was supposed to be
Which felt like déjà-vu. And then she was gone.
And now he knew how it felt to stand
On the local platform as the express whizzes by
With people chatting in a dialect
Of English he couldn't understand, because his English
Was current as of 1968 and no one speaks that way except
In certain books. So the hours spent in vain
Were minutes blown up into comic-book balloons full
Of Keats's odes. "Goodbye, kid." Tears streamed down
The boy's face. It was a great feeling,
Like the feeling you get when you throw things away
After a funeral: clean and empty in the morning dark.
There was no time for locker-room oratory.
They knew they were facing a do-or-die situation,
With their backs to the wall, and no tomorrow.

Last Words

"Enough." "No, more." "Not me," he said, closing the door,
Walking away from the blaze in the bedroom behind him.
"I'm going straight." He could barely see. The sun was blinding.
Yet he knew they would come for him—it was only a matter
Of time. "Mama," he called, though the personage thus named
Was dead, and had been dead for decades, an ocean away,
In another city, another land. A stenographer was on hand
To record his last words. "I don't need a priest," he said.
Then the lights went out. It was the old familiar thrill
Of homesickness all over again. The slow earth churned on

And the money—the money was gone. Gone like *that* (he snapped
His fingers). Gone forever. And so, after the longest delay
In the history of the Trans-Siberian Express, the landscape
Began to rumble forward, just as the old fool said it would.
Europe was still the biggest bloody thing in North America.
There were no more plans. They had all turned into hospitals.
And there was nothing left to eat or smoke. A dream of tomorrow,
A prayer to an absent deity, what difference did it make?
He couldn't remember how he got here or who he was,
Only that he was still alive—that was the miraculous part,
And nothing she did would change his mind. She licked her lips.
"More," he said, liking the sound. "More, more, more!"

The Choice

He had to choose. He could fight the Vietnam War
In a helicopter rescuing diplomats from Saigon
In his dreams or in the air-conditioned tomb
He and his wife had been living in since April—

Or he could refuse in favor of a love affair
With a woman who swam the English Channel
Using two strokes. She had high cheekbones and jet black hair,
Or maybe it was foxy eyes and a mop of brown curls.
Anyway she had infiltrated his dreams.
He lowered his voice. "War and peace may be great themes,"
He said, "but adultery is even greater."

It was their last conversation in bed.
"You're going to miss me," she said,
"Kiss me," he heard,
And the prediction began to come true
With her voice still in his ear.

"Sometimes what you thought was an interruption
Turns out to be your life.
And sometimes what you thought was your life
Turns out to have been an interruption.
And yet you have to act
As if you were back in the fourth grade
And knew the right answer was Pittsburgh
But put down Bethlehem just to see what would happen—
How it would feel to be wrong."

Dark Passage

He said he missed the city. He meant he missed her
And her habit of bumming cigarettes, showing up late,
Looking rich. It was no wonder he couldn't remember
Her face in the morning, or the name of the country
He was in, or the exact nature of his mission. He was
Afraid that if he looked at her, he'd lose her, but
He couldn't help himself. And she looked back
With the largest saddest eyes he had ever seen.
Then she was gone, swallowed by an oceanic crowd,
A Mardi Gras crowd full of pickpockets and thieves,
And the distance between the lovers kept widening,
And he kept calling her name. The ocean spewed her out
On a foreign shore. Some people wore masks.
Everyone had drunk too much wine. It was dark,
And the tape in the bistro lasted sixty minutes,
So he had now heard "These Foolish Things" in French
Seven times, only this time someone else was with him,
Whose face he never gets to see. Sleep this once
Came speedily. His ambition was lofty.
She said she meant him. She really meant anyone.

On the Run

"Too late," said Uncle Alvin, checking his watch.
He was supposed to take the boy to the funeral,
Little suspecting it would be his own. *Too late*:
The killing words. "'But, my friend, we have come
Too late,' said the hero." The textbook salesman
In the motel room can hear the words echo
In his ear, and wonders what they mean in *his* case:
Has he left something undone? Neglected someone
He should have loved? More than likely. Yet
Even at twenty-eight, years before the age of regret,
He had already heard the words. It was too late
To assemble the birds as he had pictured them
One spring morning. Too late to marry the girl
And sire numerous offspring in bohemian splendor.
Too late for anything but life on the run, life
As he was living it, in motels and rental cars,
Running away from something, though not sure what,
Running in place, to keep up with the others,
In pursuit of the ring rolling down the street
Or to escape into the glory of an unknown destiny.
Running into enemy territory, as fast as a boy.

A Little History

Some people find out they are Jews.
They can't believe it.
They had always hated Jews.
As children they had roamed in gangs on winter nights in the old
        neighborhood, looking for Jews.
They were not Jewish, they were Irish.
They brandished broken bottles, tough guys with blood on their
        lips, looking for Jews.
They intercepted Jewish boys walking alone and beat them up.
Sometimes they were content to chase the Jew and he could elude
        them by running away. They were happy just to see him run
        away. The coward! All Jews were yellow.
They spelled Jew with a small *j* jew.
And now they find out they are Jews themselves.
It happened at the time of the Spanish Inquisition.
To escape persecution, they pretended to convert to Christianity.
They came to this country and settled in the southwest.
At some point the oral tradition failed the family, and their
        secret faith died.
No one would ever have known if not for the bones that turned up
        on the dig.
A disaster. How could it have happened to them?
They are in a state of panic—at first.
Then they realize that it is the answer to their prayers.
They hasten to the synagogue or build new ones.
They are Jews at last!

They are free to marry other Jews, and divorce them, and intermarry
    with gentiles, God forbid.
They are model citizens, clever and thrifty.
They debate the issues.
They fire off earnest letters to the editor.
They vote.
They are resented for being clever and thrifty.
They buy houses in the suburbs and agree not to talk so loud.
They look like everyone else, drive the same cars as everyone else,
    yet in their hearts they know they're different.
In every *minyan* there are always two or three, hated by the others,
    who give life to one ugly stereotype or another:
The grasping Jew with the hooked nose or the Ivy League Bolshevik
    who thinks he is the agent of world history.
But most of them are neither ostentatiously pious nor excessively
    avaricious.
How I envy them! They *believe*.
How I envy them their annual family reunion on Passover,
    anniversary of the exodus, when all the uncles and aunts and
    cousins get together.
They wonder about the heritage of Judaism they are passing along
    to their children.
Have they done as much as they could to keep the old embers
    burning?
Others lead more dramatic lives.
A few go to Israel.
One of them calls Israel "the ultimate concentration camp."
He tells Jewish jokes.
On the plane he gets tipsy, tries to seduce the stewardess.
People in the Midwest keep telling him he reminds them of Woody
    Allen.
He wonders what that means. I'm funny? A sort of nervous
    intellectual type from New York? A Jew?
Around this time somebody accuses him of not being Jewish enough.
It is said by resentful colleagues that his parents changed their
    name from something that sounded more Jewish.
Everything he publishes is scrutinized with reference to "the
    Jewish question."

It is no longer clear what is meant by that phrase.

He has already forgotten all the Yiddish he used to know, and the people of that era are dying out one after another.

The number of witnesses keeps diminishing.

Soon there will be no one left to remind the others and their children.

That is why he came to this dry place where the bones have come to life.

To live in a state of perpetual war puts a tremendous burden on the population. As a visitor he felt he had to share that burden.

With his gift for codes and ciphers, he joined the counter -terrorism unit of army intelligence.

Contrary to what the spook novels say, he found it possible to avoid betraying either his country or his lover.

This was the life: strange bedrooms, the perfume of other men's wives.

As a spy he had a unique mission: to get his name on the front page of the nation's newspaper of record. Only by doing that would he get the message through to his immediate superior.

If he goes to jail, he will do so proudly; if they're going to hang him anyway, he'll do something worth hanging for.

In time he may get used to being the center of attention, but this was incredible:

To talk his way into being the chief suspect in the most flamboyant murder case in years!

And he was innocent!

He could prove it!

And what a book he would write when they free him from this prison:

A novel, obliquely autobiographical, set in Vienna in the twilight of the Hapsburg Empire, in the year that his mother was born.

The Secret Life

She was strange. Even as a child she had been able
To picture her own death, as a prisoner pictures freedom.
The first time they met, he walked her to her third-floor walkup
On a city landmark block, tiny but with a lot of light.

The first time they went to bed, Mahler's Fourth Symphony
Was on the record player. They traded insults, had a fight
To juice themselves up for the main event, and in the morning,
Her guilt and his anger were gone. Neither of them could remember

The reason for the delay: hadn't their analysts explained
The loss of his wallet, her keys, that weekend at the shore?
The last time they went to bed, both of them knew it;

The neighbors knew it in the morning when her mother came
To collect her things, and her father mentioned his lawyer.
He felt like a burglar in his own living room when they left.

It started in the subway in Boston, where he thought he saw her
Before he knew who she was. The Red Sox were scheduled to play
Oakland that night at Fenway, but it rained all day
And he went to see a Hitchcock double feature instead.

He met her there, in the second half of *Vertigo*
And the first half of *Rear Window*. Afterwards they walked.

Neither of them was hungry, and both of them
Had something they wanted to keep quiet about.

He kept comparing Grace Kelly and Kim Novak in his mind,
Wondering about the woman he was with, and how little
He knew about her. Was it enough to get him to follow her

Into the Spanish church with the high tower
Where he was sure to have a dizzy spell
At dusk, after he rescued her from drowning?

Every time she left him she took off her wedding ring,
Slammed it on the dresser top, stormed out. Four hours later,
Sex was better than ever. They stayed up late to watch
The debonair husband bring his fragile wife a glass of milk.

Had he put poison in it? Or was it just his wife's bad nerves?
Clearly, *he* got on hers. She said he was too contentious.
They could never just enjoy a movie like ordinary people,
They had to analyze it to death. One day she locked herself

In the bathroom, sobbing, saying she had taken a lethal dose
Of Dalmane. It wasn't true, but he believed her, and made her drink
The vile stuff prescribed by the emergency-room guy on the phone.

She was scared of him, and basked in the fear, egging him on
To see him lose his temper while she kept cool and sarcastic,
Playing the role of the bitch, knowing how much he liked it.

As phone sex is to sex, so was their strained dialogue
To the quarrel they should have had. He brought up the baby.
All she could think of was the casserole in the oven.
She rehearsed the day's doings: X made a pass at her, Y frowned

When he said good morning, and Z is up a creek because
Her boyfriend has AIDS. He listened with one ear tuned

To the Mets game on the radio, down six to four in the eighth
But with the bases loaded and HoJo at the plate. Ball one.

He kept turning over sentences in his mind: "Her husband
Never suspected, not because he was dense but because
It hadn't occurred to him that other men might desire her

As he did not." And, "Maybe she needed to treat herself
To a breakdown, or maybe just a glass of water and a pill."
Every time he left her, he phoned her two days after.

Should she listen to his shrink sessions on tape, which
He had left behind—deliberately, she supposed?
Her shrink would have called it "an accident with intent,"
On the grounds that there were no accidents, no errors,

No false prophets or dreams, no mistakes that weren't messages
From the unconscious, texts for her to interpret and complete.
The tapes were meant for her ears only. Love abolished ethics:
That was her philosophy, and she would take it into the street

And see what happened. The prospect exhilarated her. Here at last
Was a project commensurate with her energy, her fanatical zeal
To do good works and get her hands dirty, be among the people,

Until she heard his voice on tape, going on and on about his moral
Dilemmas. His feelings had changed. He didn't want to hurt hers.
All this talk about feelings . . . She wanted to slug him.

He brought up the baby, which was strange because
They didn't have a baby. She tried to reason with him, but
Humoring him was smarter. He was mixed up. One drink too many,
An extra toke of extraordinary grass. No appetite, no sleep.

His lawyer explained how he could cheat her. He got indignant.
"I don't want to cheat her," he said. His lawyer sighed,

"It's your funeral." His favorite expression.
The object of the game was to make the ball disappear.

They checked in. He asked for a double room
With a king-sized bed. "You're very sure of yourself,"
She said, when the clerk went to get the key.

Raindrops in the sun, on the windshield, on the roses,
Blackening their crimson; on her cheek, a tear; in the air,
The trace of her giveaway smile in the getaway car.

She used to visit him before he knew who she was,
What she looked like, and why she came to him
At night, when the others were asleep. And now . . .
Was it possible? Was she the same woman

Framed in the window's tall landscape
Of pine trees receiving the evening's blue powder?
He had thrown away the frame, wanting her to enter the picture,
And he would go there with her, down country lanes

In France, where the pears were ripening
In poems of pleasure that had not yet been written,
For he could imagine an embrace as fierce as the one she fled from,

As cold as the taste of snow on burning lips,
And was prepared to love her in a shabby unlighted corner
Of the attic, on the shortest day of the year.

Dutch Interior

He liked the late afternoon light as it dimmed
In the living room, and wouldn't switch on
The electric lights until past eight o'clock.
His wife complained, called him cheerless, but
It wasn't a case of melancholy; he just liked
The way things looked in air growing darker
So gradually and imperceptibly that it seemed
The very element in which we live. Every man
And woman deserves one true moment of greatness
And this was his, this Dutch interior, entered
And possessed, so tranquil and yet so busy
With details: the couple's shed clothes scattered
On the backs of armchairs, the dog chasing a shoe,
The wide-open window, the late afternoon light.

The Theory of the Leisure Class

In theory the sky was gray all that winter in London: no central
    heating, a constant drizzle, your feet were constantly cold.
In practice it was the same old overheated New York City apartment
    —but once you went outside, how near the sky, how blue.

In theory a man watching as a woman dresses, slowly, slowly, for the
    benefit of his gaze, is a man to be envied.
In practice he needs a shave.

In theory a man choosing among three women—his past wife, his
    future wife, and his current mistress—chooses the mistress.
In practice he is choosing among the daughters of King Lear.

In theory the revolver in the desk drawer was not meant to be used—
    it was a prop in a play, to be brandished once or twice by the
    hero in a fit of temperament.
In practice the newlyweds soon discovered the limits of their tolerance
    for each other's quirks.

In theory it was a trip to the places on the postage stamps in the
    collection I had as a boy: Magyar Posta, Ceskoslovensko,
    Jugoslavija, Deutsches Reich, Österreich.
In practice it was the experience of examining a 1957 Duke Snider
    baseball card fifteen years later, and noticing how young
    Snider looked. He hit forty home runs that season, the
    Dodgers' last in Brooklyn.

In theory she was the right woman at the wrong airport. It was the
    first time he had seen her without her makeup.
In practice, she wears flats and never comes into Manhattan without
    having stockings on. Watching her walk in front of him, the
    auburn-haired man in the dark shirt and tie calculates the
    exact relation of danger to desire.

In theory the passengers are irate. "You are inept," an owlish-looking
    gentleman hooted at a red-faced customer service agent.
    Two cops turn up and the unattended shoe box in the TWA
    ticket area becomes the object of lively discussion. Then the
    announcement is made. Everyone has to clear the area—it's a
    real live bomb scare, folks.
In practice you take a cab into the city and notice for the first time the
    little shopfront at Lexington Avenue and 94th Street: Chao's
    Laundry. Remove the apostrophe and you arrive at your chosen
    destination. The adrenaline automatically starts to flow.

In theory the voice of authority is never heard—the word unspoken is
    what commands us.
In practice I was having lunch with an executive in the publishing
    industry. He said that success in management meant "having
    not only the responsibility but also the authority." Later
    I heard the same phrase from the general manager of the
    San Francisco Giants and from a guy I know in middle
    management in Rochester. I figured it must be true.

In theory a man does his best work under the pressure of deadlines
    and production schedules.
In practice a man does his best work on a beach in Bermuda, on an
    exceptionally clear October day, followed by rum swizzles at
    sundown and a little night reading.

In theory the woman was absent.
In practice every inch of the canvas implicated her in the man's idle
    fantasies of leisure and success.

Stages on Life's Way

1. The Night Before

He liked waiting. Waiting gave him a purpose to live.
Waiting outside the marriage counselor's office,
He read that the unconscious is structured like a language.
The verbs in the dream he had the night before were

Copulating on flying carpets or chasing taxis in Tokyo,
Always doing something, taking action, not just waiting
As he was doing now, waiting quietly in an armchair holding a book,
Or pacing back and forth like an expectant husband,

Waiting for the appointment with the insignificant clerk
Without whose signature the elopement would be cancelled,
Waiting without anxiety, knowing that the time of the wait

Would be infinite and how much clear thinking could be done,
Waiting for the dinner bell, for the music to begin,
Waiting for the fog to lift, so the darkness could be seen.

2. The Morning After

"You're a bastard," she said,
Admiringly. He was; he admitted it. He saved his own book
From the flames, letting hers burn. How young he looked!
She spat: "I'd rather be dead."

The ritual began with a kiss, as it always did.
The one-armed man identified himself. "My name," he flashed
His teeth, "is death." And the fruit in her mouth turned to ash
In the darkened hotel room, under the coverlet.

A ringing phone interrupted their embrace.
She put a hand to her face.
Where had he seen her before? In somebody else's window.

The woman in the painting was somebody else's widow,
Somebody else's wife.
But that was art, and this was life.

   3. The Next Day

He was impulsive. One day he decided to read Conrad
And bought *The Secret Agent*, *Victory*, and *Under Western Eyes*.
The next day he had a craving for canned fruits
And came home with purple plums in heavy syrup, Queen Anne
   cherries

In light syrup, and pineapple chunks in juice, no sugar added.
Also, he wasn't going to the theater enough, so he lined up seats
For *Gypsy* and *City of Angels*. Then he forgot to go, and left
The cans of fruit in the icebox, and put Conrad on the shelf.

The next disaster hadn't yet begun. So there was time
To find out what she was like as a child, and they could be
Children together in her parents' hotel room, opening the drawers,

Hiding in the closet, and she put on her mother's pearl necklace,
And later they looked for snakes behind bushes, and she fell down.
It was summer: a bowl of ripe apricots, the mud on their knees.

The End of the Affair

1.

It may have been what she wanted all along:
An episode in a foreign film, Swedish or French,
Where the taciturn man and woman in the hotel lobby
Have their last chance to act nobly, stoically,
Before they are separated by the fortunes of war,
And each forgives the other, and neither is to blame.

Or it may have been what she wanted all along:
The intoxication of paranoia, where the suspicion is mutual,
And she doesn't know what he does for a living,
And he knows that her last two lovers died violent deaths.
It was like the rush of inspiration that only a nervous breakdown
Can give you: she looked at the roses and burst into tears.

2.

It was as if she had brewed a supremely powerful pot of coffee
For breakfast, and he watched as it transported her
To Paris and the smell of bakeries in May, and she watched
As he went back to the day he noticed something different
About his wife, her hair or a new silk scarf she was wearing,
That made him realize she was having an affair. It was almost

Like being inside a snow-filled paperweight, which someone shakes:
It was snowing, he won't forget, and she told him
He made her feel beautiful in the snow, and what he wanted
Was what he thought he wanted—delight in the body
Sleeping next to his, the curve of her back, the barrette
That fell out of her hair as she slept.

from *Operation*

Memory (1990)

Pascal's Wager

1.

The thunder altered everything, starting with the shape
Of the sky. It had once been flat. Now, like the earth,
It was round: the concave part of the spoon,

A mirror in which everything was upside down.
The system of mirrors between the sky and the lake
Was a mistake, like music without sound.

The echo lasted into the night and sounded like thunder.
"I have come to give you the key that opens no doors,"
Said the prophet. And the stars turned black in his honor.

2.

The patron saint of lost causes bids me to be religious.
The argument is melodious, seductive.
Religion is based on the revelation that it's over.

Religion and lamentation are one, and therefore
The elegy is the most religious of poetic forms.
Churches attract us as monuments do. In France

We went to Chartres and Amiens and Reims and Rouen,
All the grand cathedrals. They meant more to us
Than the royal gardens or the castles along the Loire.

3.

But at the inevitable zinc bar of a bright café
Where Blvd. Montparnasse meets Blvd. Raspail,
Somebody figured it out. The insurmountable problem

Of religion in the twentieth century was:
How you gonna keep 'em down on the farm after they've seen
Paree? So, for a time, it survived among us out of habit,

Objects of nostalgic desire: the prayers
You said when you went to bed as a child,
The songs your father taught you, the words.

4.

The repetition of words: there was the poetry of scripture,
The same stories with added emphasis every year:
The story of Joseph, my father's name, the story of my own, David.

Beauty of ritual, discipline, ceremony:
The cup of wine and two loaves of bread on Friday night,
And the double candlesticks glowing in the dark.

There was the sense of being part of a collective destiny,
Hurt by our enemies into history. There was
The morality of the survivor, and the memory of thunder.

5.

Faith, from the beginning, resembled gambling. Every prophet
Is a gambler at heart. In the casino of the imagination,
You would meet the true believers at the roulette wheel

Or green-felt tabletop, where the dice came up seven.
The jackpot was a group portrait of angels
In heaven, which you admired for its representational exactness

Though you felt in your heart that representation
As an aesthetic principle was dead. In abstract art
Lay the future of an illusion, thirty years ago.

6.

Europe was more innocent, not less, than the United States
When we discovered it. We brought the danger and anger
Of New York sidewalks with us, and the freedom.

On the battlefields of Belgium, religion meant row after row
Of crosses in the thick October twilight. Religion was death
Or somebody else's misfortune. Imperialists of the imagination,

We smuggled Greek statuary—proud, erect, nude—
Into the cathedrals we entered like railway stations,
Suitcases in hand, in Paris and London and Madrid.

7.

The result was predictable. Sex became a species
Of religious worship. We heard the arguments against it,
The injunction against idolatry and so forth,

But couldn't resist the logic of our position.
The athlete and the aesthete were one.
There was even the sense that pornography

On blue summer evenings was religion by other means.
Our favorite café had turned into a cave, in the south of France,
Where stalactites of strange and wondrous shapes surrounded us.

8.

Then they put a gun in my hand. They made me
Carry a lit candle as I sleepwalked in the dark.
I walked in my sleep every night for months.

My dreams were listed on the index of forbidden books.
In the darkness I went in my canoe, for you. I sent messages
From "Totem Pole" to "Love Box" with my ham radio

Assembled from parts purchased by answering an ad
In a comic book. My soul was entertained
By the knowledge of its ignorance. Art meant indifference.

9.

Indifference to suffering, except your own: not a very noble
Formula, yet one in widespread use. The poet
Of sensations affirms many things. Pleasure, desire,

Fulfillment, happiness, and joy are the five points
Of his star. Yet in the emptiness of night,
Until our eyes get used to the darkness, the lit candle

Of the sleepwalker is what we need to see by
As we make our way forward, afraid of the dark
Yet more afraid of standing still, wandering into nomad's land.

Perfidia

You don't know who these people are, or what
They'll do to you if you're caught, but you can't
Back out now: it seems you agreed to carry
A briefcase into Germany, and here you are,
Glass in hand, as instructed. You rise to dance
With the woman with the garnet earrings, who is,
Of course, the agent you're supposed to seduce
And betray within the hour. Who would have known
You'd fall in love with her? Elsewhere the day
Is as gray as a newsreel, full of stripes and dots
Of rain, a blurred windshield picture of Pittsburgh,
But on the screen where your real life is happening
It is always 1938, you are always dancing
With the same blonde woman with the bloodshot eyes
Who slips the forged passport into your pocket
And says she knows you've been sent to betray her,
Or else it is seventy degrees and holding
In California, where you see yourself emerge unscathed
From the car crash that wiped out your memory,
Your past, as you walk into a gambler's hangout
On Sunset Boulevard, in a suit one size too large
And the piano player plays "Perfidia" in your honor,
And the redhead at the bar lets you buy her a drink.

One Size Fits All: A Critical Essay

Though
Already
Perhaps
However.

On one level,
Among other things,
With
And with.
In a similar vein
To be sure:
Make no mistake.
Nary a trace.

However,
Aside from
With
And with,
Not
And not,
Rather
Manifestly
Indeed.

Which is to say,
In fictional terms,
For reasons that are never made clear,

Not without meaning,
Though (as is far from unusual)
Perhaps too late.

The first thing that must be said is
Perhaps, because
And, not least of all,
Certainly more,
Which is to say
In every other respect
Meanwhile.

But then perhaps
Though
And though
On the whole
Alas.

Moreover
In contrast
And even
Admittedly
Partly because
And partly because
Yet it must be said.

Even more significantly, perhaps
In other words
With and with,
Whichever way
One thing is clear
Beyond the shadow of a doubt.

With Tenure

If Ezra Pound were alive today
    (and he is)
he'd be teaching
at a small college in the Pacific Northwest
and attending the annual convention
of writing instructors in St. Louis
and railing against tenure,
saying tenure
is a ladder whose rungs slip out
from under the scholar as he climbs
upwards to empty heaven
by the angels abandoned
for tenure killeth the spirit
(with tenure no man becomes master)
Texts are unwritten with tenure,
under the microscope, *sous rature*
it turneth the scholar into a drone
decayeth the pipe in his jacket's breast pocket.
Hamlet was not written with tenure,
nor were written Schubert's lieder
nor Manet's *Olympia* painted with tenure.
No man of genius rises by tenure
Nor woman (I see you smile).
The tenure committee did not show shine
on Gertrude Stein.
Picasso came not by tenure
nor Charlie Parker;

Came not by tenure Wallace Stevens
Not by tenure Marcel Proust
Nor Turner by tenure
With tenure hath only the mediocre
a sinecure unto death. Unto death, I say!
WITH TENURE
Nature is constipated the sap doesn't flow
With tenure the classroom is empty
    et in academia ego
the ketchup is stuck inside the bottle
the letter goes unanswered the bell doesn't ring

Spontaneous Combustion

Under the mattress was a day-old newspaper rolled into a scroll,
And in the scroll was a small fortune in banknotes.
They all went up in smoke. First the sheets caught fire,
Then the mattress, the newspaper, the money. Finally,
The bed itself began to rise, ascending to the heights
Of a wandering cloud suspended between rival promontories
In the Alps. The bed disappeared into the cloud and then,
And only then, could the lovers be seen
For the first time, in the splendor of their absence,
As if a blaze of lightbulbs had outlined their bodies
In the midnight sky, just to the north of the archer.

It was as if the boy had stayed in the big store
After it closed for the night, had hidden in the men's room
When the lights went out and the clerks went home,
And all at once became aware of music in the darkness,
And crept out to witness a masquerade ball of mannequins.
That dancer, there, in the slippers and pearls! He wanted her
And would have her if only . . . if only her body weren't just
A function of the mind that designed her dress and never
Entered the nave of her nudity. And yet . . . and yet the body
Shedding that dress was real, and equipped with the lips
And hair angels lack: the proof lay there beside him
In the bed. A lover of paradox, he turned away
From the big bright cancellations of night
That announced the new day, and let sleep overcome him,
Him and her, in the levitating bed, in the flames.

The Survivors

1.

Thanks to the truth serum, no one forgot
The exact spot where each of us was standing
Waiting for an accusation, an explanation, or a miracle
Like suspects gathered in a gloomy drawing room
When the phone rang, as we knew it would,
And Uncle Joe gave his orders with his customary brevity
Forbidding us to answer the door. There was a knock.

The condemned man waited while we deliberated
Behind closed doors. The thermometer said zero
Though the truth serum made it July 1934.
He stood at the door, shivering in the cold,
With the patience of a child who lives in parables
And knows he will never enter the house.
There was a knock. We thought it was the police.

There was a knock. But no one was there when we looked.
Back on the phone, my sister Joan tried to sound reasonable.
All we had to do was answer a riddle: name the caller
Who visits you only when no one is home. "The fate
Of an innocent man depends on your reply," said Uncle Joe.
"There's no need for him to die." Could we
Have saved him with a lie? In any case, we didn't.

2.

Suddenly it was as though observation were action,
The one form of action that fatalism allowed
Since it left one's innocence intact or
Cloaked it in skepticism: and we who had always meant
To believe in the will stood helplessly by
Like relatives of the deceased, listening to lawyers deny
Our right to contest the old man's testament.

So it was decided: history had already happened,
And all we could do was watch a batch of old film clips
Chronicling the catastrophe: armistice signings
In railway cars, barbed-wire borders,
The stunned faces of the American soldiers
And the grinning skeletons that greeted them where
They had dug their own graves: and here

Was one who had escaped in the night
And crawled and then walked and then ran in the night
Until he reached a nearby farm and knocked on the door
And stood there, wondering whether he'd be saved,
When a shrill voice from behind the shut door
Uttered its unequivocal reply: Jew, go back to your grave.
It was, thanks to the truth serum, July 1944.

3.

The corpse on the operating table shakes itself back to life.
"We knew we had three wishes only
And had to save up the third
In case we goofed with the other two
And needed to become children again."
Our hero refuses to understand, though prodded by
A blind man with a revolver in his hand.

Our hero, who wasn't always a hero, lives
In despair, but pretends not to care.
He disagrees with reality. That is his right,
And he has scars to prove it. Switch off the light
And he will follow the slowest most voluptuous curve
Between any two stars, elaborating the distance
Before spanning it in a leap of forgetfulness.

The note he left in invisible ink was held to the light
Two days too late. Yet he survives the cause of his distress,
Lifts his former bride, still in her wedding dress,
And declares the weight, by a miracle of logic,
To agree with the dictionary definition of time.
Merely to have carried it was a moral action,
However futile, whatever the merits of the fiction.

The Answering Stranger

1.

Here is your childhood: a boy running.
I have cold hands. Mother, may I stay at home today?
On the radio the Japanese are bombing Pearl Harbor
In the middle of a football game. The phone rings.
"You either live too long or die too young,"
The caller says. "That's why you need insurance."

You either live too long or die too young—
Nothing else is real, not even your childhood.
Here is your childhood: a man running,
A boy running down the rungs of the fire escape,
A man driving his car through a stop sign,
An ambulance siren, your first naked body.

2.

Father forgives his enemies, but first he sees them hanged.
Mother is waiting for the knock on the door. Nobody
Is the stranger on the other side of the door,
But nobody is the wiser: a single lie explodes
The testimony given under duress by one

Who saw it all, was there, and suffered
The heightened sensitivity of a bug strutting up and down

The keyboard. "Everything I do
Is an experiment," he thinks. And therefore
He throws people off trains, or blows them up in Arabia.

3.

The anesthesia did wonders for Father's memory.
It seems that everyone in the audience is talking about him,
Though he doesn't exist. A single lie explodes

The rose, which expands to fill the entire room.
I heard the footsteps. You can't tell me the house is empty.
The caller says, "That's why you need insurance."

The big blonde in the dormitory blames her bad orgasms on Daddy.
The bearded bully puts the blame on Mame.
I am writing this not for you but for them,

The invisible others, waiting for the phone to stop ringing.
The boy who saved you from drowning says,
"Here is your childhood: cigarettes in puddles."

4.

The important colonel ordered the false confession.
A bugging device had been planted in the chandelier.
"Please extinguish all smoking materials," the role model says.
She welcomes you to the twentieth century.

The Twentieth Century is the name of a train that no longer runs.
The bomb in the briefcase goes off, but the tyrant survives
And the train no longer runs. I heard the footsteps.
I saw the footprints. But the path led only one way.

The captain turns on the landing lights.
A fire broke out in the cabin.

Yet I keep waiting for the knock on the door.
Nothing else is real, not even the ashes.

Everywhere I go I can smell the fear.
Nothing is real, not even the ashes
Of the boy who saved you from drowning
Or the stranger on the other side of the door.

Listen closely or you won't hear, though
A bugging device has been planted in the chandelier,
Which expands to fill the entire room.
Here is your childhood: a boy running.

"Please extinguish all smoking materials," the role model says.
I am writing this not for you but for her,
The naked girl dancing on the roof, who welcomes you
To the twentieth century, though she doesn't exist.

Rejection Slip

"Oh, how glad I am that she
Whom I wanted so badly to want me
Has rejected me! How pleased I am, too,
That my Fulbright to India fell through!

The job with the big salary and the perks
Went to a toad of my acquaintance, a loathsome jerk
Instead of me! I deserved it! Yet rather than resent
My fate, I praise it: heaven-sent

It is! For it has given me pain, prophetic pain,
Creative pain that giveth and that taketh away again!
Pain the premonition of death, mother of beauty,
Refinement of all pleasure, relief from duty!

Pain you swallow and nurture until it grows
Hard like a diamond or blooms like a rose!
Pain that redoubles desire! Pain that sharpens the sense!
Of thee I sing, to thee affirm my allegiance!"

The audience watched in grim anticipation
Which turned into evil fascination
And then a standing ovation, which mesmerized the nation,
As he flew like a moth into the flames of his elation.

The Desire for Strange Cities

1.

Each street means something other than it says.
On Haste Street in Berkeley, the temptation to amble
Down the hill, lazy as a guitar imitating the rain,
Is irresistible, and on Blake Street, a few blocks away,
The cross streets have names like "Jerusalem" and "Thel,"
Or they should. Meanwhile, on 74th Street in Manhattan,
Between Amsterdam and Columbus, it shall always be 1974.

2.

So tell me: in which city do you imagine yourself
And what do you imagine yourself doing
At the moment when, without warning or apology,
The world comes to an end? Variant: imagine
The circumstances of your own death. Assume,
No doubt erroneously, that death occurs only
When we have readied ourselves for it and that
We do this in our dreams. In the dream you have
All cities and all time zones to choose from.
Where will it be—at an oyster stand near
The intersection of two broad boulevards in Paris,
A London club in 1850 or a Viennese coffeehouse
Fifty years later? A smoky upstairs bedroom in the Casbah?
Getting off a bus in Jerusalem, at night?

                                        I saw myself
In Vienna, where I've never been, walking on a street
Much like the rue Soufflot in Paris. I swear I saw
Lightning while the sun was out, and it gently rained.

        3.

The traveler regaled us with stories, touching and true,
About the people he had met on his sojourns
In strange cities. Better yet were the stories
Edged with menace: the sense that something odd
Was about to happen in the railway station in Milan,
And it did, only his train had long since departed
And he was nearing Geneva when the bomb in Milan
Went off; or the story about the corpulent man,
Bewigged and wearing a judge's black robe
At La Coupole in Paris, over a café crème one morning
In 1977, who confided to the table at large
That news of Elvis Presley's death would be
Reported a week later—which happened,
Thus quickening interest in the corpulent man,
Who had disappeared in the meantime. But best of all
The traveler's tales were the ones he made up—
No, not made up, recalled—of cities
Where he had never been: sinister Berlin and seedy Sofia,
The carved portals of Vienna in its brilliant light,
Copenhagen during an unseasonably warm December,
Rio, Buenos Aires, Haifa, Hong Kong, Prague.

Mythologies

I.

The question is not how like the animals we are
But how we got that way. We laugh, for what is a suicide note

But the epitaph of an emotion? Few of us die out in the open;
And when you say thesis, I say antithesis,

But we don't stop there: we take our opposing ideas,
Plant them on opposing cliffs and then build a footbridge

Between them, seemingly flimsy yet sturdy enough
To support a battalion. Hidden behind trees, we watch

The soldiers march across it, single file, too scared
To look down. We cheer them all, all except the boy

In the fairy tale who knew no fear. Him we pity.
He laughs open-eyed, ready to die as we were not.

He is one of us, all right, but better, stronger, stranger.
He asks for more fear than anyone can bear.

II.

The guilty had three choices: awkward chords of candor,
Canned laughter, or the wild hyacinth's sutra, before

Silence returned triumphant, and the journey resumed
In darkness, though the sky above was classically blue.

Everyone kept his opinion to himself
As harmony dictated, and effigies of Tristan and Isolde

Accompanied their stubborn footsteps across the wild
Terrain. Yet the longing for a loud catharsis

At night renewed their pain. "If only we could climb
Out of these clouds and heartfelt headaches,

Like ravished children in the glory of a snowball fight
After school, and never again have to descend,

Who would not abandon these erotic shipwrecks
And fall asleep like tigers in the destined heights?"

III.

At a festival of conceptual art in Cairo,
I saw a tank buried entirely in snow.

I knew then that silence is the source
Of all music, all laughter, all thought, and so

I stuffed pebbles in my mouth and stood by the sea
And roared my defiance of the waves. It was here,

Years before, that our plane and its shadow
Converged: I ran from the fire, carrying the flames

In my arms. I ran and ran, feeling like a man
Fighting a newspaper on a windy beach, but it wasn't

A beach at all: the sand beneath me was snow,
Is snow, and the spears in the desert sky look like stars.

In the pyramid's triangular shadow, I was the man
Who heard the crimson explosion, and ran.

IV.

Keats in one of his letters says, "My Imagination
Is a Monastery and I am its Monk." I wonder.

If a man's imagination is his monastery,
This place looks a lot like an empty railway station,

King's Cross in London or the Gare St. Lazare in Paris,
A place whose smoke and fog Monet dissolved

Into a chorus of colors. There we stood, my love and I,
Having made our vows under the suspended clock,

Hero and bride. But as we walked away, side by side,
Down the station's sunless nave, amid the excitement

Of the crowd, and foreign languages spoken loud,
We knew our exile had already begun, could hear

The conductor's shrill whistle, could see the light
At the end of the tunnel, where it was always night.

V.

Paradise was hardly what Psyche
With her bleeding blackberries and nervous orgasms

Could have foretold, enjoyed,
And renounced for the sake of some querulous abstraction

Designed to keep us unhappy but alive.
Call it civilization. Call our disobedience instinctive.

Or say we obeyed an angry muse, who ordered us to dance.
"Or else?" I asked. She sighed before answering.

"Or else a dismal armchair will be your lot
With chamber music your sole narcotic—music that will make

You face your former self, and grieve over incidents
Scarcely recalled, and eat without pleasure, and drink

Without thirst, and dread what shall never come to pass."
In the revelation of our nakedness, we danced.

VI.

"A ball that is caught is fuller, by the weight
Of its return, than the same ball thrown." Our empty hands say so.

We feel free. In the other room the true believers remain,
The ones who insist that evil is real, the only real thing.

Cannibals and missionaries they are, accomplices in sin,
Greedy for punishment, to inflict or endure it.

We are glad to leave them behind, glad not to have to hear
Their chants and wails. Down the elevator we go

And out into the canyon created by skyscraper shadows.
Yet even we, dedicated as we are to good living,

Sometimes walk around with a lost look on our faces,
As if the blessing for a piece of fruit or cup of wine

Had suddenly come to mind, though cup and plate are empty;
Had come to mind and faded almost instantly away.

VII.

Admit it: you used to walk around thinking there had
To be a reason for things, for everything. That way

Paranoia lies. Not a science of syllables, the solitude
Total, but the prophet's lit lantern was what you wanted—

And what you got was "neon in daylight," a pleasure
Recommended by Frank O'Hara. Those pleasures meant a lot to you,

You even thought you lived for them, until the first death
(A nervous uncle broke the news when you landed at Kennedy)

And the first marriage (you stayed up all night and read
Beyond the Pleasure Principle, a fair description

Of your lovemaking). It seems that new myths are needed
And consumed all the time by folks like you. Each erases the last,

Producing tomorrow's tabula rasa, after a night of dreams
In which the tigers of wrath become the tigers of repose.

VIII.

Go back to the beginning, to the first fist fight.
They played for high stakes those days. The penalty for losing

Was death or slavery, take your pick. To spare a life
Was the mark of the master; the mark of his slave

Was fear. Noble savage, nothing. Forget about paradise.
My vote goes to Hobbes's "life of man, solitary, poor,

Nasty, brutish, and short." An amazing sentence:
The syllable that ends it also lends it its poignancy,

Since we go on wanting what we can scarcely bear.
Go back, go back, back to when god became a swan

With beautiful wounded wings, and raped the astonished maiden.
Back to the dream that stays real when you wake up,

Accustomed to your hunger and clinging to it,
Like a panther accustomed to his cage. Go back.

IX.

A slap in the face, and the face burns with shame.
Anger comes later, comes stranger, looking for someone to blame.

End of message. Can't see the stars;
Can't say anything that hasn't been said before

By somebody slamming the door; can only repeat
The syntax that brought the crowd to its feet

In the silence that appeased the nightingale.
End of tale. But its moral was simple:

I lost the hearing in one of my ears
And listened with the other to a deaf man's

Symphony. He built a heaven out of his fears
That there wasn't one. End of nightmare.

—The imperfect past, going by too fast,
Begged us to collect it. It couldn't last.

X.

The doctor put his cards on the table.
"Take your pick," he said. He was able

To offer me fear of extinction or fear of pain,
Though freedom from neither. "You mustn't complain."

In the vertiginous air, the monks wore masks
To keep their germs to themselves and their

Identities a secret. A hero to his own valet,
The Sultan choreographed his murderous ballet

Until Scheherazade, entering the circus tent
With John the Baptist's head on a silver tray,

Told her tale and made the crowd repent.
The curtain dropped and the crowd went on its way,

But no one could say what the nightmare meant,
Or why it was sent to us, or by whom it was sent.

XI.

You can't have it, so you want it, or
You couldn't have it, so you no longer want it, or

You're stuck with it, forever. It was designed with you in mind,
Like the locked door that swung open majestically when you

Spoke the magic words or just answered in the affirmative when
Your name was called. "Here I am, ready to meet you,

Ready to make any sacrifice," you said,
Still in bed, wrestling with an evil angel

In your sleep. You were seventeen years old then
And woke up with a limp. Desire is like that:

The girl knows what you want and cries when
She gives it to you because it was yours because

She whispered your name in your sleeping ear
And said: "Here I am." And was gone a minute later.

XII.

I met her in one of those sleazebag bars—
I think it was called The Bottom Line—in Buffalo,

Self-proclaimed "city of no illusions," where
Silent men in shirtsleeves sit on bar stools and watch

Girls with tattoos on their buttocks strip
Down to G-strings and pasties. They dance to the thump

Of moronic music, grind and hump under hot strobe lights,
And then, when the act is over, circulate among the scumbags,

Gyrating in front of each in turn, making each feel special,
And each, aroused by the mingled smell of musk and sweat,

Folds a dollar and sticks it into her crotch for a tip.
She was different. When I left the bar that night I knew

She would follow, and she did, and I never looked back, never
Glanced at the rearview mirror. All other women turned into her.

XIII.

Her name is Mary but was Miriam before that and soon
She will change it to Alice. What she offered was a shadow

The shape of Europe on the map above the bed of my youth.
Her shawl is all that remains of Europe in the downstairs closet.

It was forbidden to lift up her skirt and look, look.
Yet boys and girls danced across the bridal morning like a bridge

As the wings of the fog like white sails lingered
Across the bay. I flew, like a caterpillar with wings, into the new day.

That was the day we buried Europe. We cubed the square
But failed to save our fares. To hang like a spider

On a subway strap seemed a suitable fate for some, but we
Lit a candle and watched it cast the shadow of a mountain

In a valley. "I'll be there, I'll be dodging shells; I won't be fighting,
But I'll be running like hell." It was all over, except for the writing.

XIV.

In the dream of your choice, you wake up
In the Garden of Eden, alone except for a whore with a heart,

Wearing a nurse's uniform. The serpent says:
Listen carefully. This is for your own good.

At the tone it will be eight o'clock.
Nine out of ten physicians recommend

That you surround yourself with the kind of sorrows
That can be instantly relieved by frivolous kisses,

With vegetables as lush as fruits
Ripening in your hands. When the hospital gates are opened,

Don't hesitate, run! And when you arrive at last in the land
Of the free, take your place in line with all of the others

As though nothing had happened between then and now
To make you doubt the conviction that you're blessed.

XV.

If you were a painter, you'd paint the wind
Green. It would shake the boughs of the honey locust trees.

It would chase the leaves across the continent.
It would scatter crumbs in a twist of swirling snow.

It would be colorless and green at the same time,
The wind that aligns the pond and the cloud,

The wind that is everywhere, in constant motion,
As buoyant as Ariel and as scornful of gross Caliban,

The wind that holds up the fly ball, drives it back
Into fair territory, causes it to drift within reach

Of the rightfielder, who waves off the second baseman,
Until a last gust lifts the ball over both their heads

And it lands safely for the double that ends the game
In extra innings, costing our team the pennant.

XVI.

After the flood, refreshed, was the first time
You realized that the road to truth was the road

Of flagrant fiction. You surrounded yourself
With symbols (a mountain, a window, an ark,

A rainbow) and mythic creatures (the dove that returned
And the raven that didn't). You understood the dream

233

Of the old woman who interpreted the sailor's dream.
Then came the other birds, the clouds that come

When the rain is done, and the wind that signals
The discovery of dry land, a new continent,

As the report of a gun sounds the start of the race,
As the glass broken beneath the bridegroom's foot

Begins the marriage, as church bells start the funeral
Parade and all the townspeople march in the procession.

XVII.

No longer is there freedom in confusion,
Nor forgiveness in confession,

Nor charm in the old illusion
Of moonlight, the tower, the howling dog, the escaping lovers,

Escaping into midnight in the Western hemisphere,
When the possibilities of expansion still seemed limitless

And the soul could choose among stars without number
In the vast velvet night without end.

—In the midst of other woe than ours, I went to the window
And cured the solitude of the listeners outside

Who shivered in the rain, waiting for the police to come
And ambulance sirens to sound. Drunk I was when

I went to the bathroom, looked in the mirror, and said,
"Dad, Dad, is that you?" In the terror of the night.

XVIII.

"Wherever you follow," he said, "I will lead."
Where summer met fall, she picked up a brittle orange leaf.

He wanted to lie on the grass, to lean and loaf
At his ease, but the crisis intervened: news of her unpaid loan

Prompted him to put his sandals on his head, as in the Zen koan.
Slowly he walked away. Silence followed, then the sound of a moan

In the room next door. So orange it seemed a painted moon
Shone against the indigo sky. And quickly her mood

Went from unreasonable euphoria to realistic dejection, as the wood
In the fireplace turned to ash without first yielding a flame. The wool

Of their sweaters had begun to unravel. "If the fool
Persists in his folly," someone said, "he will have food

Enough to eat, loaves and fishes galore. Worship the good,
Which is beautiful though untrue. Turn your back on gold."

XIX.

If we were painters we'd favor vibrant stripes,
Primary colors, flat surfaces, a lot of white

Remaining on the canvas. If we were composers
We'd take the music of exotic jungles with us

When we visit the vast vacant tundra. "If I were
Rich enough," vowed the philanthropist, "I'd move

To a magnolia mansion and spend my days
Translating modern literature into ancient Greek."

Great plans, distant vistas, a rearguard action
To sabotage the present—and here we've all assembled,

At the antiseptic airport, with haunted looks on our faces.
Occasional eye contact between man with tan and woman in white.

"You look like your voice," she says, breaking the silence.
The rest of us know where we're going, but we don't know when.

XX.

They've cornered the market on moral outrage. Yes, they have.
The more noise they make about it, the more nervous we get.

They're always telling us just how shallow we are.
The only convictions we have, they say, are on our drivers' licenses.

The charge is not entirely fair to us, though it has its grain of truth.
We tend to luxuriate in our indecisiveness. Not they. No one can say

They lack conviction and passion and certitude. We have our doubts,
Which make us less glamorous and give us

The haunted look we wear. But something in defense
Of our bemused spectatorship must be said: at least it spares us

The postures of those hypocrite lechers, brothers and others
Who sublimate their sexuality into opulent rhetoric and chide us

For not doing the same. They have our best interests at heart.
They may even be happier than we are. We have our doubts.

XXI.

Today's graffiti is in the sky: "More than meets the eye."
Growing up I could tell the months by their smell.

First come the fruitstand smells of spring in the city,
Then the backyard trees get back their green, and we know

It's the real thing. Poetry in this puzzle of missing parts
Is best represented by clouds in the early evening sky,

Because they constantly change shape, are utterly indifferent
To us, and seem both remote and near at hand

At once. The creation of the world is a ballet
With the dancers and music missing: what you see

Is a miniature stage-set in a museum display case,
And then suddenly you are walking in it, along the boulevard Raspail,

Until the Eiffel Tower comes into view. Watch it organize
The bridges of the Seine into a coherent surprise.

XXII.

Love accompanies the stranger to his streetlamp
Encircled by singing insects. The song he hears

Meant doom or wax in the mariners' ears.
And now, as the smell of fresh cut grass gives way to the smell

Of brown leaves burning, I want to tell
You what I heard that night, and how the day

Erased it: I woke to the rattle of a passing car
Which, accelerating up the rapidly rising ramp,

Seemed delighted with its capacity for making noise. From far away
I could hear it coming. And just as we know that fame isn't all

It's cracked up to be, that it can be downright
Nasty in fact, and yet we want it anyway,

So I, too, knew I belonged in one of those cars, tall
Behind the steering wheel, racing to meet the changing light.

XXIII.

Winter came last. Waves of snow from who knows which wind
Turned the meadow beside the frozen waterfall

Into an ocean. The boy in the fairy tale who knew no fear
Soon learned. On the shore of the wide world he could hear

The violins of anger, spelling danger. Poetry in this era of disbelief
Meant staring at a leaf until it turned into a star.

It was easier in the past. All you had to do was sleep outside
And let nature take over. There were more stars in the sky

Than we had room for in our philosophy. And when we woke,
Berries grew beside the burbling brook and bled in our soft hands.

The question was not how like the gods we were
But whether we could recognize them in our sleep

And remember what we had seen, remember them clearly,
When the radio alarm welcomes us into its next musical day.

XXIV.

I live in a boat in front of the door
Depicting the gods as they might have been forgotten

By Lazarus during the tortures of interrogation.
What I see are tombs and yellow stains on the snow.

Instead of quotations, I will refer to my heart;
Instead of an altar, I will guard the munitions

And drink wine with the sour taste of cork
And eat sour strawberries in the city of New York.

You who've been looking for a lost address,
And mothers who seem to be fighting back their tears,

What made you think you could resist the roar
Of the years as they echo in a cavernous subway station?

Can you see the boat in front of the door?
What was it you forgot during the interrogation?

XXV.

Ovid had it wrong. The plight of the frightened maiden
Gliding noiselessly into the woods, like a deer whose eyes

Had been mesmerized by headlights on a cold November night,
Was implausible without the contrivance of arrows: love's dart

Claimed Apollo while the dart of fear pierced Daphne's heart,
And so she ran, deeper and deeper into the woods, losing ground

All the while to Apollo (for love moved faster than fear),
Until the gods, granting her wish, turned the nymph

Into a laurel, which Apollo hopelessly embraced. Poetic justice?
Yes, except it didn't happen that way. Their foot race ended

In a forest clearing, where Daphne, exhausted but unashamed,
Made Apollo watch her undress. He entered her

At her request, as if his will were an extension of her own.
The trees, inclining their branches, nodded in consent. Love won.

XXVI.

The boy, who was more eager than his father
To live on a raft, sleep in the woods, and study the stars,

Became his father, but not before he hid in a cave, slept in it
Overnight, and was saved by a spider from sure destruction.

The king's soldiers, hot on his trail, saw the web stretch unbroken
In the mouth of the cave, and assumed that no one was there.

What is the correct interpretation of the spider's web?
To the soldiers it meant desolation; to the spider, conquest;

To the grandfather telling the tale, providence. The boy
Sees the dew cling to the web at dawn. The natural camouflage

Of rabbits and snakes isn't lost on him. He notices
The triangle formed by three birds in the bare-branched sycamore.

He can hear the hum of a bee admiring a tulip's genitalia.
And at night, he knows, all the colors are present in the white of the stars.

XXVII.

That was the year I first read Hölderlin.
The evening fell more slowly and the first day of spring

Arrived more suddenly and stayed lovelier longer.
Boys pursued muses and girls impersonated them.

With the instinct of insects, He and She on the meadow
Mate. What they dreamed stays real when they wake up

In the evening of the first day of spring.
Did they fall out of paradise or were they pushed?

240

It's unclear, but we next see them enter the gathering dusk,
Hand in hand, and the camera pulls back and the voice-over says,

"Good fortune is even harder to bear
Than the bad fortune that came first. Remember this

About the gods: their own immortality suffices them.
The source of all rivers is a riddle even I cannot solve."

XXVIII.

How little I have changed since then, or how much
Of the change is in the eyes of the beholder

Of a book I lived rather than wrote, whose author
Seems like a stranger to me today. I remember,

For example, wanting to write an apocalyptic parody
Of Milton, in Milton's high style, titled "Eden in Flames."

Adam and Eve celebrated their carnality, and when they woke,
The branches of the fruit trees curved gracefully down

And served them nectar. I couldn't bring myself to describe
Their banishment, and so the project failed. Yet what I heard

When I slept sounded a lot like the chorus of joy
In Beethoven's Ninth, and what I saw when I woke up,

If only for the length of a dream, was a deer,
Eyes mesmerized by headlights, motionless in the middle of the road.

XXIX.

You could be the only passenger on the bus
Who notices that the driver is blind. I, by contrast,

Have eyes only for lovely you. Give me your hand.
I will kiss it. You are cordially invited to my studio,

Which resembles a psychiatrist's office. Once there, I put on my glasses,
Read passages out loud from Plato, Hobbes, Marx, and Freud,

And ask you for your opinion of each. Together we analyze
Solitude. There is a meeting of the minds,

And sex follows. It's the first day of spring, and we want
To walk along the river and roll on the grass and take off

Our clothes while leaving the windows wide open. In fact,
We can't wait to get off this bus, which seems to be going

Nowhere fast, as Spring puts her tongue in my ear
And names the forbidden parts of her body.

XXX.

No one could say what the nightmare meant
In the operating theater or the circus tent.

And none of this will help us pay the rent:
Many are called and sleep through the ringing,

But we know it's spring, though we've thrown our watches away.
Our dreams, stretching across the chasm of day,

Don't deter us from waking, jumping into our clothes,
Dancing down the avenue, and swinging through

The revolving doors of the future, where we used to live,
The day before yesterday, when we weren't dying.

242

—The question is whether the raven will return
After his end-of-the-world adventures, after the storm,

When one by one the masks slip off, and the bride embraces
The guilty son: true to the test, remembered and confessed.

Operation Memory

We were smoking some of this knockout weed when
Operation Memory was announced. To his separate bed
Each soldier went, counting backwards from a hundred
With a needle in his arm. And there I was, in the middle
Of a recession, in the middle of a strange city, between jobs
And apartments and wives. Nobody told me the gun was loaded.

We'd been drinking since early afternoon. I was loaded.
The doctor made me recite my name, rank, and serial number when
I woke up, sweating, in my civvies. All my friends had jobs
As professional liars, and most had partners who were good in bed.
What did I have? Just this feeling of always being in the middle
Of things, and the luck of looking younger than fifty.

At dawn I returned to draft headquarters. I was eighteen
And counting backwards. The interviewer asked one loaded
Question after another, such as why I often read the middle
Of novels, ignoring their beginnings and their ends. When
Had I decided to volunteer for intelligence work? "In bed
With a broad," I answered, with locker-room bravado. The truth was, jobs

Were scarce, and working on Operation Memory was better than no job
At all. Unamused, the judge looked at his watch. It was 1970
By the time he spoke. Recommending clemency, he ordered me to go to bed
At noon and practice my disappearing act. Someone must have loaded
The harmless gun on the wall in Act I when
I was asleep. And there I was, without an alibi, in the middle

244

Of a journey down nameless, snow-covered streets, in the middle
Of a mystery—or a muddle. These were the jobs
That saved men's souls, or so I was told, but when
The orphans assembled for their annual reunion, ten
Years later, on the playing fields of Eton, each unloaded
A kit bag full of troubles, and smiled bravely, and went to bed.

Thanks to Operation Memory, each of us woke up in a different bed
Or coffin, with a different partner beside him, in the middle
Of a war that had never been declared. No one had time to load
His weapon or see to any of the dozen essential jobs
Preceding combat duty. And there I was, dodging bullets, merely one
In a million whose lucky number had come up. When

It happened, I was asleep in bed, and when I woke up,
It was over: I was thirty-eight, on the brink of middle age,
A succession of stupid jobs behind me, a loaded gun on my lap.

Fear

The boy hid under the house
With his dog, his red lunch box, and his fear
Thinking God is near
Thinking it's time to leave the things that mean
Just one thing, though you can't tell what that is,
Like God or death. The boy held his breath,
Closed his eyes and disappeared,
Thinking No one will find me here—

But only when his parents were watching.
When they weren't, he slipped away
And hid under the house
And stayed there all night, and through the next day,
Until Father (who had died that December)
Agreed to come home, and Mother was twenty
Years younger again, and pregnant with her
Darling son. Hiding under the house,
He could see it all, past and future,
The deep blue past, the black and white future,
Until he closed his eyes and made it disappear,

And everyone was glad when he returned
To the dinner table, a grown man
With wire-rim glasses and neatly combed hair.
Fear was the name of his dog, a German shepherd.

New York City, 1974

1.

"They're invisible and God is blind," Ron says I said,
And it seemed like the right answer at the time
Though neither of us remembered
What the question was. "Every dead man has one
Phone call coming to him," I'm alleged to have added
The night Ali knocked out Foreman in Zaire
On the radio of some upper Broadway bar
Known only to the two of us, and the inevitable femme fatale
Who sidled up and said, "My monkey's wild," meaning
Whatever. Whatever worked: that was the principle
Behind our cryptic aphorisms, haikus that refused
To be epigrams. Byron played first, Shelley second, and Keats shortstop
On my Romantic all-star team, with Billie in the background
And Ron reading Rilke aloud, as we collaborated
On the typewriter in his Eleventh Avenue living room where
It was always three a.m. Godard met Miss America and asked,
"Are drugs a spiritual form of gambling?" I was on an espresso high:
"My heart is jumpin', you started somethin', with them there eyes."

2.

Spend a few hours here and you start talking to yourself,
Like everyone else in the joint. The American idiom
Was a beggar in the bathroom menacing a sophomore with a toy gun:

"Do you got a piece of candy for me? A stick of gum? A cookie?"
If everything is evidence, everything is admissible,
And my tape recorder proves it. I'm thinking of the cabbie
Who turned around, apropos of nothing, and snarled:
"You know what I seen? Blonde girls, blue-eyed beautiful, sucking
        nigger cock *for a dollar*."
He italicized those last three words. I wrote it down, I wrote
Everything down, as though it would otherwise disappear,
As though everything was meant to end up in a book.
And Jamie was sleeping with Amy and I with Beth,
Or maybe it was the other way around.

        3.

Auden was asked whether he believed in free love.
"Surely, if it isn't free, it isn't love," he said.
And if it *is* free, it isn't money,
So Ron and I signed on to write filler for a book called *Future Facts*
About the wondrous things the future had in store for us
Like a vaccination against syphilis
And voice detectors to fight crime
And how shit could be recycled into food
For astronauts. I filed away the formula somewhere, or Ron did.
The boss wanted upbeat quotations for the margins. The day I quit
I brought in Orwell: "If you want a picture of the future,
Think of a boot stamping on a human face—forever."
The boss said: "That's not what I want to see in the future."
"But what you want to see and what you will see aren't necessarily
        the same,"
I replied, more interested in a good parting shot than the truth,
Unless fear was the truth and the truth could kill you.
Nana accused me of wearing an affected nonchalance, and I agreed,
        reasoning that
Irony was the best defense against the threat of extinction,
Which I felt daily, for no good reason, and which made sex sexier
In New York, the capital of my mind, in 1974.

4.

I lived with Ed and Josh and Jamie.
Ed had been to Vietnam with the marines and screamed in his sleep
And told stories about savage drill instructors
And said, about the latest in a long line of lovely skirts,
"I'd dribble a basketball through a minefield for a sip of poison from
    her well."
He was from Virginia and Josh was from California
And memorized Chinese ideograms while watching *Chico and the*
    Man,
Eating peanuts and throwing empty beer cans at the TV.
During commercial breaks, Ed held forth over dinner:
"The following individuals should be executed immediately,"
    followed by
A list of politicians celebrities TV anchormen and his own former
    bedmates.
We were drunk. Jamie, all charm, played Bud Powell at the piano
When he wasn't reading *The Naked and the Dead*
And imitating Marlon Brando in *The Godfather,* the greatest
    American film since *Citizen Kane.*
Neither of us knew what he wanted to do with his life.

5.

Nor did anyone else. I took a job ghosting the autobiography of an
    elderly lady
Who turned out to be an amnesiac. Then a graduate student at
    Columbia
Asked me to translate a book of poems from the Greek and when I
    said I didn't know Greek
She said it didn't matter. Recent Barnard graduates and Radcliffe
    graduates, oh,
And French teachers and German teachers and actresses disguised as
    waitresses
And nurses and editorial assistants and dancers who lived on West 83rd,

Amy Beth Carol Doris Elaine and Fran,
In love with you, with all of you, I am, can't help myself, feeling
Like a dog at the mercy of his tongue, unable to think straight,
And I was going to edit a literary magazine called *Young Lust*
But didn't because an impatient finger pressed the up button
Five times in one minute, waiting for the elevator to come
And lift me to her penthouse apartment
Where she twisted her nude body like a discus thrower.

6.

It was she, my nameless blonde asthmatic goddess, who
Told me the story, a Russian fairy tale, about
An old man climbing a beanstalk carrying his old wife
In a burlap bag. As he nears the hole in the sky he'd carved
With his penknife on a previous trip, he slips
And, fighting to regain his balance, drops the bag,
And his wife breaks up into numerous bones,
And we next see him crying on the ground next to the bag of bones.
She didn't say how the story ends, but you can guess. He wanted her
And she wanted him, and from behind the tree an effigy
Of Eve emerged, holding out an apple in her hand. Both
Of them ate greedily. It was the tree of forgiveness.

7.

Somewhere in this city there's a Kafkastrasse
Though you can't tell where it is, mustn't look too hard,
And are bound to get lost on the journey, as we did.
Got to keep going: between the arrow and its target were
An infinite number of detours, and we wanted to take them all,
Take them wherever, as long as we're together, humming along.
Take the A train. Item: a drunkard falls on the subway tracks,
And the teenage boys who rescue him promptly lift his wallet.
Item: Steve and Rita, moving to San Francisco, parked their packed car
In front of my building and came up for a goodbye cup of Bustelo.

By the time they went back down, twenty minutes later, all their stuff
        was gone,
The windshield smashed, and the vandals had raided the oil tank
To decorate the seats: Ron called it the New York touch.
What I like about this city is
The background music, one hundred percent pre-bop jazz,
The girl on the bus whom you will never see again,
Gray dawn, the fog lifting, the buildings renewing their assault on the
        sky,
The Empire State Building like a giant injection,
And history is being made but like the biography of an amnesiac
It's a different fiction every day, image yoked violently to image,
And literature comes to life: Hamlet crosses the street
And is hit by a car for his impertinence. That was freedom,
A car speeding through a red light at 100th Street and Broadway.
The body covered by a raincoat remained in the gutter
Long after the crowd dispersed, went home, went to work, went to
        sleep.
How did it happen? They were invisible and God was blind.

Cambridge, 1972

1.

Rob B. came in, chuckling. He had found the quintessential
    Beckett short story.
It began: I was young then, feeling awful.
Then Larry came over with his list of suicidal poets
And everyone decided to write a poem in the form of a suicide note.
Mine ended: And that's what they're going to find in my pocket
    tomorrow morning, folks.
It was an imitation of Mayakovsky's last poem but
I don't remember how it began. Charlotte came up
And took off her clothes as soon as Larry and Rob stepped outside
To fight it out over Sandra, who stayed in London awaiting the
    results.
Charlotte's terms of endearment include: my pet, my duck, and my
    chuck.
She was Australian and smoked jasmine cigarettes. Rob B. was
    South African
And kept picking up the girls everyone else fell in love with.
Rob A. was a Californian via Yale who ran a 4:10 mile
And borrowed my leather vest which I still have and which I
    should have given him.
We were best friends and when I returned to America he moved in
    with Charlotte
After explaining what Marcuse meant by "reification" and
    "repressive desublimation."

252

Larry said: "I want to be the poet of Detroit." Then Sandy came
     over with some hash
And made tea and showed us how to win against the Sicilian Defense,
And we all went to the Arts Cinema to see *Wages of Fear.*
When we got there we realized we didn't remember how.

2.

God's name was an audible image at ten o'clock. At eleven Donatello
     revived the great bronze nude.
At noon we chose among Auden's adjectives. Charlotte voted for
     "clever hopes."
I liked "habit-forming pain." Then we went to the Eagle or the
     Pickerel
And drank a pint of Greene King and ate Scotch eggs. Alan came
     Over and said, "What
Do you think of this?" and read us a twenty-page short story
     called "A Girl Named Tweedy."
I said it was a very good title. Then Lew came by fresh from
     Paris in his blue velvet suit
With Becky the piano girl at Fagin's. Lew thought Joan Miró was
     a woman.
The literary magazine came out and it had eleven poems by eleven
     different poets
Each titled "The Old Man." Professor H., introducing Robert
     Lowell
At a poetry reading, called him "one of the greatest living poets"
Adding: "And I think we can safely remove the word 'living' from
     that description."
He meant it as a compliment, but Lowell looked ashen-faced.
At the Round Church, a symposium: Does God Still Wear a Blazer?
Next week: The Vertigo of Relativity. And the week after:
"Imagination is reason in her most exalted mood."

3.

Rob B. wrote a poem called "The Real America," never having been
    there.
Sandy in his Kant phase took a walk down Trinity Street, turned into
    Clare, crossed the Cam
And headed back over the Mathematical Bridge at three sharp every
    day.
His Wittgenstein period came next. Larry said, "Here's another
    suicidal poet
I think you'll like" and read me the poems of Pavese.
I was in my Groucho Marx period and Lew was in his Frank Zappa
    period
And Charlotte was in her Ginger Rogers period and Larry was in
    his Motown period.
I translated the prose poems of Henri Michaux, my favorite being
    "Simplicity"
In which the poet takes his bed with him whenever he goes outside.
If a woman passes by and catches his eye, why, he takes her to
    bed immediately.

4.

I remember the Brussels sprouts and boiled potatoes, the one
    Cornish hen supposed to feed fifteen
At the house of the Clare chaplain, who visited the rooms of the
    seriously ill.
The dog walked in and peed on the carpet and the chaplain's wife
    Said, "Oh, Rosebud, you're being boring."
Boring meant something other than boring. When the word came up in
    Uncle Vanya
The whole audience burst into laughter. But we all looked
    solemn in the chaplain's house.
The food itself looked famished, especially the vegetables.
Rob A. came over and the lights went out because of the coal
    miners' strike.

I was on page 523 of *The Brothers Karamazov* and we talked about
        Dusty (we called him Dusty)
And Nietzsche (who never did betray the heart that loved him).
Then Eve came over, who looked like Ingrid Bergman in *Notorious*,
And Alan came over with his tennis racket.
And Hillary came over and complained that Cambridge men were
        impotent
And I wore jeans with a tweed jacket and wide paisley tie
And Lew married Joyce who became a radical lesbian in Arizona
And Charlotte married a laconic French engineer who wore suits
        from Ted Lapidus
And Rob A. went to Canada and Rob B., back to South Africa,
And Sandy is still smoking his pipe and making Lapsang souchong tea
And Larry is explaining how Sam Cooke was shot to death,
As we get into the cab that will take us to the station
Down to London, to Heathrow Airport, to return to the United
        States.

For I Will Consider Your Dog Molly

For it was the first day of Rosh Hashanah, New Year's Day, day of
    remembrance, of ancient sacrifices and averted calamities.
For I started the day by eating an apple dipped in honey, as ritual
    required.
For I went to the local synagogue to listen to the ram's horn blown.
For I asked Our Father, Our King, to save us for his sake if not for
    ours, for the sake of his abundant mercies, for the sake of his
    right hand, for the sake of those who went through fire and
    water for the sanctification of his name.
For despite the use of a microphone and other gross violations of
    ceremony, I gave myself up gladly to the synagogue's sensual
    insatiable vast womb.
For what right have I to feel offended?
For I communed with my dead father, and a conspicuous tear rolled
    down my right cheek, and there was loud crying inside me.
For I understood how that tear could become an orb.
For the Hebrew melodies comforted me.
For I lost my voice.
For I met a friend who asked "is this a day of high seriousness" and
    when I said yes he said "it has taken your voice away."
For he was right, for I felt the strong lashes of the wind lashing me by
    the throat.
For I thought there shall come a day that the watchmen upon the hills
    of Ephraim shall cry, Arise and let us go up to Zion unto the
    Lord our God.

For the virgin shall rejoice in the dance, and the young and old in each
    other's arms, and their soul shall be as a watered garden, and
    neither shall they learn war any more.
For God shall lower the price of bread and corn and wine and oil, he
    shall let our cry come up to him.
For it is customary on the first day of Rosh Hashanah to cast a piece
    of stale bread or, in my father's family tradition, a stone into
    the depths of the sea, to weep and pray to weep no more.
For the stone represents all the sins of the people.
For I asked you and Molly to accompany me to Cascadilla Creek,
    there being no ocean nearby.
For we talked about the Psalms of David along the way, and the story
    of Hannah, mother of Samuel, who sought the most robust
    bard to remedy her barrenness.
For Isaac said "I see the fire and the wood, but where is the lamb for the
    offering?"
For as soon as I saw the stone, white flat oblong and heavy, I knew
    that it had summoned me.
For I heard the voice locked inside that stone, for I pictured a
    dry wilderness in which, with a wave of my staff, I could
    command sweet waters to flow forth from that stone.
For I cast the stone into the stream and watched it sink to the bottom
    where dozens of smaller stones, all of them black, gathered
    around it.
For the waterfall performed the function of the chorus.
For after the moment of solemnity dissolved, you playfully tossed
    Molly into the stream.
For you tossed her three times, and three times she swam back for her
    life.
For she shook the water off her body, refreshed.
For you removed the leash from her neck and let her roam freely.
For she darted off into the brush and speared a small gray moving
    thing in the neck.
For this was the work of an instant.
For we looked and behold! the small gray thing was a rat.
For Molly had killed the rat with a single efficient bite, in conformance
    with Jewish law.

For I took the rat and cast him into the stream, and both of us
    congratulated Molly.
For now she resumed her noble gait.
For she does not lie awake in the dark and weep for her sins, and
    whine about her condition, and discuss her duty to God.
For I'd as lief pray with your dog Molly as with any man.
For she knows that God is her savior.

From *An Alternative*

to Speech (1986)

Enigma Variations

1

Sir Winston Churchill advised against suicide
"Especially when you may live to regret it."
After an endless faculty meeting at Princeton,
Einstein revised his theory of eternity.
"Just a run in time's stocking," said Nabokov.
The child grows older while everyone around him
Stays the age they were when he was born.

The painter and his model change places.
The nude wears a mask. Otherwise she is nude.
Otherwise she is just like all the other passengers
On this hijacked jet suspended over Manhattan.
One terrorist says: Let the death be as illuminating
As the resurrection. Everyone else has frozen
Into the age they were when he was born.

2

Let the alcoholic transcend his religious upbringing.
Let the Leaning Tower of Pisa stabilize its tilt.
Let the spaces between Pollock's *Blue Poles*
Vibrate with the music of the spheres and
Let the death be as illuminating as the resurrection,

And as beautiful. A million degrees centigrade:
The sun's corona during a total eclipse.

If the world has terrors, said Rilke, then
We must learn to love them, for they belong to us.
Notice the "if." If among all these skeletons
One stood up to denounce his tormentors
Crying "We shall outlive them!" in triumph as if
His escape did not mean his destruction:
The sun's corona during a total eclipse.

3

The driver of the hearse seen from the hospital window
Says, "There's room for one more inside,"
And so does the bus conductor the next afternoon.
We know it will crash, but it's our destiny
And we can't escape from our destiny, though
We refuse to climb aboard. A used syringe was found
In the toilet in the back of the bus.
They would never have permitted it in the hospital.

The lovers dreamed in parallel lines that converged
When they woke up, midway between heaven and no place.
I was the blind painter who could see his model
Only by touching her. We met on the bus
Which didn't crash, except when we were asleep
And we could see the place exactly as it was
Except that we were missing from the picture.
They would never have permitted it in the hospital.

4

Terror links the father, the son, and the sacrificial ram.
Thanks to a choice typo in *Time*,
The Allies snatched victory from "the jews of defeat,"

The chosen people, who live across the street,
Having babies and working for a living.
The law requires a medical examination before execution:
The law of self-preservation, which doesn't exist,
If we can commit suicide and live to regret it.

The terror of transgressing angels, looking homeward,
Is ours, because there's no one else to blame.
We are the chosen people, choosing to laugh
At a practical joke that isn't all that funny.
The Appian Way is now Highway 7, and Icarus
In his plane need fear no more the heat of the sun
As he flies, fatherless, midway between heaven
And no place: a suicide who lived to regret it.

Glose

Let our frail thoughts dally with false surmise.
In trenches big enough for two lovers and a machine gun,
I changed chance into a synonym for the sun.
No, not one, but many skies.

With a shrill whistle the referee called time
And back to the bench they went, their previous triumphs forgotten,
Their pious guilt remembered, by generals bereft
Of a reasonable war. I changed chance into a rhyme
For *more*: light less light less than a little light was left.
Under the circumstances, did it pay to advertise?
Seduced by the words,
The sky was filled with the absence of birds.
Take off your glasses. Take me by surprise.
Let our frail thoughts dally with false surmise.

Open your eyes. When the birds of February escape
Into March, and the trees prepare to don the disguise
By which alone they can be recognized, I shall change chance
Into an idol, and break it. Reluctant to change shape,
The caterpillar slinks away. The cobra consents to dance.
It's already hard to remember who won
Though the peace has just begun. Suspending our disbelief,
Perhaps we'll see the career of a tree in a single fallen leaf.
Don't bet on it. There's work to be done
In trenches big enough for two lovers and a machine gun.

Close your eyes. Obeying laws of its own,
The elevator will stop on every floor, its steady rise
Inevitable. On every floor a different century
Clicks into place. Thirty seconds—and then it's gone.
With our bandaged binoculars, what could we see?
In an age of poverty, what could be done?
I shall divine your every wish,
The waiter says, proffering the dish
Of pearls and amethysts he has chanced upon.
(I changed chance into a synonym for the sun.)

The anxious son, pride of the parish, dies in a capsized canoe.
The nude resumes her place on the couch, now that the revolution,
Like a boulder swallowed by the ocean,
Has ended in a splash seen by no one. Such falsehoods run true
To form. Is "lose" the opposite of "find"—or of "win"?
The question has launched a thousand lies.
There is, in fact, nothing to fear
Except for the strangeness of being here
Since the sun, like a guillotined orange, has begun to rise.
No, not one, but many skies.

The Master of Ceremonies

1

The master of ceremonies wears the philosopher's hat.
Hitler was a vegetarian. Did you know that?
Alexander the Great drank too much. And Jonah
My Jonah didn't want to go to Nineveh,
No matter what people say. He'd have slept instead,

But the sword of Damocles hung over his Procrustean bed,
Which wasn't the lesser of two evils. This the master
Knew, as he understood all things past or
Passing overhead, like a desert cloud. Then the Bronx
    moved downtown.
Time with a frown turned the hourglass upside down.

2

My mother admired the orange pyramids
At the fruit stand on Dyckman Street.
"And these," the proprietor said, pointing at a stack
Of shriveled ones in the back, small as walnuts,
"Are for Jews." "For juice," he really said.

For the war was over. She must have heard wrong.
The whole of the population had dressed
In sackcloth and ashes, to wail and beat their breasts.

266

"Sorry," the lady at the laundry told me.
"We don't do fewer than one shirt."

"But this isn't fewer than one shirt,"
I said, holding up my twice-worn blue Oxford shirt
With button-down collar, for her to see.
"It isn't?" she asked with a gentle smile, humoring me.
I looked at it and lo! it burst into flame.

She laughed. "I beg your pardon," she said.
"I'm laughing with you, not at you." I wasn't laughing.
The master explained the silence by clapping his hands
Once, and making a low bow. "And Nineveh still stands,"
Jonah said accusingly. "For thou art a gracious God."

3

At last the firing squad lined up. Each of the marksmen
Had dropped to one knee when—suddenly, unexpectedly—
The truth came out. His pardon had reached the warden
Several days earlier. *Just wanted to give him a little scare.*
From the shock of his freedom he would never recover.

Gift Means Poison in German

And *poisson* means fish in French.
Therefore, on my first trip to Paris,
reading a menu I recalled
my cousin, now a fashionable designer,
then a survivor of Dachau, twelve years old,
a week after arrival in New York City
when Truman was president. I thought
of what she must have thought when,
for the first time, she rode on the Broadway bus
and passed one gift shop after another.

Poison, too, is a funny word, a gift horse
given by deceitful Greeks: look in its mouth
and see: it sounds what it says, it seems.
For example, five years ago I walked
into the Jolly Corner grocery store
which no longer stands on 75th Street
and Columbus Avenue. A man and his wife,
ahead of me in line, were buying Camels for him
and Winstons for her when
a display case of brightly packaged junk food
next to the cash register caught his eye.
His wife said, in a tone it would take a gifted actress
years to perfect, "that stuff is poison!"
and then she stalked out of the store as though,
perhaps, the ongoing argument that defined their marriage
had taken a new, subtle turn. Tilting his head

toward the door, the man behind the counter
faced the abandoned husband and said
"*she's* poison." He said it as if he knew
and by god I thought he did: very possibly both of them
were right, I decided: and wondered what the husband
was thinking, who had suffered in silence
this perfect stranger to insult his wife.

Shake the Superflux!

I like walking on streets as black and wet as this one
now, at two in the solemnly musical morning, when everyone else
in this town emptied of Lestrygonians and Lotus-eaters
is asleep or trying or worrying why
they aren't asleep, while unknown to them Ulysses walks
into the shabby apartment I live in, humming and feeling
happy with the avant-garde weather we're having,
the winds (a fugue for flute and oboe) pouring
into the windows which I left open although
I live on the ground floor and there have been
two burglaries on my block already this week,
do I quickly take a look to see
if the valuables are missing? No, that is I can't,
it's an epistemological quandary: what I consider
valuable, would they? Who are they, anyway? I'd answer that
with speculations based on newspaper accounts if I were
Donald E. Westlake, whose novels I'm hooked on, but
this first cigarette after twenty-four hours
of abstinence tastes so good it makes me want
to include it in my catalogue of pleasures
designed to hide the ugliness or sweep it away
the way the violent overflow of rain over cliffs
cleans the sewers and drains of Ithaca
whose waterfalls head my list, followed by
crudities of carrots and beets, roots and all,
with rained-on radishes, too beautiful to eat,
and the pure pleasure of talking, talking and not knowing
where the talk will lead, but willing to take my chances.

Furthermore I shall enumerate some varieties of tulips
(Bacchus, Tantalus, Dardanelles) and other flowers
with names that have a life of their own (Love Lies Bleeding,
Dwarf Blue Bedding, Burning Bush, Torch Lily, Narcissus).
Mostly, as I've implied, it's the names of things
that count; still, sometimes I wonder and, wondering, find
the path of least resistance, the earth's orbit
around the sun's delirious clarity. Once you sniff
the aphrodisiac of disaster, you know: there's no reason
for the anxiety—or for expecting to be free of it;
try telling Franz Kafka he has no reason to feel guilty;
or so I say to well-meaning mongers of common sense.
The way I figure, you start with the names
which are keys and then you throw them away
and learn to love the locked rooms, with or without
corpses inside, riddles to unravel, emptiness to possess,
a woman to wake up with a kiss (who is she?
no one knows) who begs your forgiveness (for what?
you cannot know) and then, in the authoritative tone
of one who has weathered the storm of his exile, orders you
to put up your hands and beg the rain to continue
as if it were in your power. And it is,
I feel it with each drop. I am standing
outside at the window, looking in on myself
writing these words, feeling what wretches feel, just
as the doctor ordered. And that's what I plan to do,
what the storm I was caught in reminded me to do,
to shake the superflux, distribute my appetite, fast
without so much as a glass of water, and love
each bite I haven't taken. I shall become the romantic poet
whose coat of many colors smeared
with blood, like a butcher's apron, left
in the sacred pit or brought back to my father
to confirm my death, confirms my new life
instead, an alien prince of dungeons and dreams
who sheds the disguise people recognize him by
to reveal himself to his true brothers at last
in the silence that stuns before joy descends, like rain.

Ode

People in the Middle Ages didn't think they were living
Between two more important and enlightened eras;
Nor did they see themselves as the players
In act three of a tragedy in five acts.
It was not always late winter in the Middle Ages.
People in the Middle Ages were not all middle-aged
Though it is enjoyable on occasion to assume that they were.
The sun was as bright in the Dark Ages
As it is now—maybe a fraction brighter, in fact.

Think of the Middle Ages and what do you see:
Gloomy cathedrals, students dressed like monks in the rain,
Or a band of drunken pilgrims telling obscene jokes,
Or heroes embarking for the nearest wilderness come April?
Your answer will reveal yourself to yourself
But you may not know it—may choose to hide
In hazy visions of a serene and indescribable paradise.
And paradise, as we know, may be paradise when we're dead,
But is boredom on earth, alas.

We never think of ennui in relation to the Middle Ages.
Should we? Did Thomas Aquinas never get bored
Cooking up elaborate refutations of diminutive heresies?
No, and you shouldn't either. Nor did the clerks
Of Oxford tire of the sin against the Holy Ghost,
Trying to figure out what it was.

On chill September mornings when
I smoked too much the night before
And I drank too much the night before
And a sinister cough rises up
From the depths of the belly of my being,
I like to imagine living in Provence
Or even in Rheims during the Middle Ages.

The Thirty-nine Steps

Logic can take you only *to* the border, not over it.
I am sad. But I have the protection of speech.
The rest is only the first time I saw a cross
Around the neck of a uniformed girl my age
In the public library, making her strange and very,
Very beautiful. The rest consists of youth's

Refusals to take anything seriously except youth's
Reluctance to grow up and be done with it.
You are happier. Shyly, you have come to the very
Edge of finding out. But as the sergeant's brave speech
Was forgotten, minutes after, by the soldiers who came of age
During their first tour of the distant hill, the one with the cross

On top of it, so some hypothetical "he" may now see that same cross
As the genius of Christianity as art. With an innocence most youths
His age were likely to conceal, he wanted to be age-
Less rather than adult, and wondered if it
Was true, that the words of the senator's splendid speech
Meant nothing whatsoever. Did it change the chill he felt in his very

Heart? Perhaps he was the only one paying very
Close attention. These graduation ceremonies were a cross,
Usually, of the stupidly funny and the stupidly boring. The speech
Of formal gibberish, the inaccurate notion that all youths
Become men at precisely the same instant, the way it
All seemed as opaque and foolishly friendly as an adage

Or an order issued by a mother. "Act your age,"
Mine still says to me, and at twenty-eight I'm still not very
Clear as to what that means. Does it
Imply, for example, a mandatory choosing at every which cross-
Roads? Yes, tell me about the prerogatives of youth's
Decline into maturity. That would make a pretty speech,

And stripped of sermon, pep talk, and speech,
You and I are likely to feel naked, of indeterminate age,
And indistinguishable. This is the point of youth's
Indifference: the first of any new series always seems the very
Last of the series that preceded it
Into oblivion. So it must have seemed to the original cross-

Carrier before it was finished. Yet the youths
Still listened, as though to a very solemn speech,
Listened and wept, dragging the years across the backs of their age.

The Difference Between Pepsi and Coke

Can't swim; uses credit cards and pills to combat
    intolerable feelings of inadequacy;
Won't admit his dread of boredom, chief impulse behind
    numerous marital infidelities;
Looks fat in jeans, mouths clichés with confidence,
    breaks mother's plates in fights;
Buys when the market is too high, and panics during
    the inevitable descent;
Still, Pop can always tell the subtle difference
    between Pepsi and Coke,
Has defined the darkness of red at dawn, memorized
    the splash of poppies along
Deserted railway tracks, and opposed the war in Vietnam
    months before the students,
Years before the politicians and press; give him
    a minute with a road map
And he will solve the mystery of bloodshot eyes;
    transport him to mountaintop
And watch him calculate the heaviness and height
    of the local heavens;
Needs no prompting to give money to his kids; speaks
    French fluently, and tourist German;
Sings Schubert in the shower; plays pinball in Paris;
    knows the new maid steals, and forgives her.

Sonnet

No roof so poor it does not shelter
The memory of the death of at least one man
In at least one septic room,
No wind so light it dare not dislodge
From their neglected home beneath the house
The bones of a discarded belief.

Yet the buyer cannot bear to look, keeps
A lock on the cellar door, and prays
For the well-behaved past to stay in place
As if, like the date on the blackboard,
It existed only to be ignored and erased
But threatens nevertheless to endure
Beyond the hour of its chalk, suspected
If not seen, like the smudge of a star.

The More You Have to Lose

Time lies, and a year can go by in a day.
Look at your watch. Do your eyes say 2:45 at 9:15?
The more you have, the more you can give away.

You know the feeling, having no money, having to stay
With relatives when you travel, unable to say what you mean:
Time lies, and a year can go by in a day.

When my father turned into my son, as in a play,
All the fun took place offstage. What about the missing queen?
The more you have, the more you can give away.

The less you believe. The more you wish you could pray.
Like a clock without hands, the truth of a face remains unseen.
Time lies, and a year can go by in a day.

With an elbow on the counter, and no passions left to sway,
The all-night waitress smokes butt after butt, coughing in-between:
The more you have, the more you can throw away.

Ocean, what is on the other side of all that blue and gray?
What does the grass know of yesterday's vanished green?
Time lies, and a year can go by in a day.
The more you have, the more you can give away.

III

Early and
Uncollected Poems

Literal Lives

Lamb wrote a dissertation on roast pig.
Hogg and Suckling did not. Wordsworth
Was not what you would call an economical writer.
Wilde tamed London. Pater was his literary father.

Pound earned a small but steady income from his writing.
Ping-pong was Tennyson's favorite indoor sport.
No one else had done what Donne did in verse:
Erotic lyrics in a religious idiom, and vice versa.

Racine's roots went deep into France's classical soil.
The Iliad was Homer's first grand slam.
The Spanish Tragedy exemplifies Kyd's mature style.
Swift wrote slowly. Pope pontificated.

Frost wondered whether the world would end in ice.
Moore was less wordy than Longfellow, whose short poems
Are his best. Peacock strutted. Bishop
Preferred Rio to Rome and the Vatican.

Ford couldn't drive a car. Neither, of course, could
Austen. As a child Woolf adored the story of
Little Red Riding Hood. West died in California.
Mann loved women. Hardy endured.

(1989)

Nirvana

I have not yet attained nirvana.

I've eaten Cotuit oysters with Zwiec beer
And Blue Point oysters with Grolsch beer
And Chincoteague and Box and Wellfleet oysters
With San Miguel and Hofbräu and Molson and Bass
But I have not yet attained nirvana.

No, I have not yet attained nirvana.

I've devoured wickson plums in the golden state
And purple plums in the pine tree state
And shiro and greengage and kelsey plums
In the bay and ocean and granite states
But I have not yet attained nirvana,

No, I have not yet attained nirvana.

I've gathered lupins in Maine and trillium in New York
And cross-bred fuchsia with baby's breath in San Francisco,
Made a bouquet of broom and viburnum in Venice,
Studied the trumpets of azaleas, and pansies freaked with jet,
But I have not yet attained nirvana.

And I've fasted for as long as a week, drinking nothing but water,
Slept twenty-four hours without the help of a pill,
Smoked marijuana in Mexico and hashish in Honduras,

Concentrated on the clarinet to the exclusion of all other sounds,
But I have not yet attained nirvana.

I've slept with English and Swedish girls in France
And a German girl who sang Mahler lieder in London
We made love in every room of the house
And in the car and under stars and at all times of day,
But I have not yet attained nirvana,

No, I have not yet attained nirvana.

(1978)

October Classic

It gets late early here.
—Yogi Berra

"If only there were a way of knowing . . ."
but what do you want to know? The anxiety you've begun
you would miss; and the consolations of chaos
can't help but continue, aware of themselves or not,
like facts you once blasted for being
pointless, which they are, only now that is a pleasure,
that there should be something beyond doubt
and certainty, pointless as a box score
forgotten days later, but which is now, and in the meantime,
the only important thing, win or lose, bet or no bet,
freezing at Shea because they're playing the Series
at night these days, and the man next to you, in scarf
and hood, could be your own self complaining
that nothing's the same as it was

(1973)

Robert Desnos

for Ron Horning

I do not know whether a point is possible,
A new beginning, an end less arbitrary
Than my own death; but I have talked so much
Of gods, dreamed their whispering absences
So much, that when I keep silent
Those moments before death, I feel I am listening
To the listening of the gods.

(1973)

Simplicity

after Henri Michaux

That's what's been missing from my life: simplicity. Up to now, that is. Slowly but surely I'm beginning to change.

For example, these days I never leave the house without taking my bed along. If a woman passes by and catches my eye, I take her to bed immediately.

If her ears and nose are ugly or too big, I remove them with her clothes and stash them under the bed, ready for her to take when she leaves; I keep only what I like.

If she would benefit from a change of undergarments, I arrange it. It's my gift. If, however, a prettier woman walks by, I voice my regrets to the first and make her disappear without delay.

Some people who know me claim that I can't do what I've just described, that I haven't got the balls. Well, that may have been true in the past, but that was because I wasn't doing everything *exactly the way I like it.*

Now I always enjoy my afternoons. (Mornings I work.)

(1972)

from "Goodbye Instructions"

1.

We are waiting—all of us—for that immense
Something to take place. What is it?
Flames . . . we are all waiting
For the flames to take place. So we can applaud.

So we can extinguish them. So we can teach you,
You, who are a girl—have you ever understood
Why? That boy was dying on the stage
For you. Why? Like a soldier. Dance around him

With your eyes. Everyone applauds. You hold
The flames in your eyes. You can hold them
Like flowers—only brighter—in your eyes.

You can drown them with your love, while
We are left waiting. Or wear them as a disguise.
The curtain comes down. Everyone applauds.

And you are the only dancer left. Look at yourself.

2.

They're real. —Those angels you spent
half your life searching for
are real. You decided. Isn't
that enough? And they're surrounding the bed,

just as they're supposed to,
at night, escorting your last nightmare away.
They're happiest at night. You can
see them at night. They want to be seen.

And yet . . . even you had to forsake them
at dawn, when with one eye closed,
you comprehended the full of the sun

with the other. And all that remained was their singing
and white dancing, which you composed.
Your friends looked on—the ones you always wrote about—

So that in the future each would say: He saw angels.

3.

A dream in which I fell . . .
I couldn't explain it.
To whom? You, whose name woke me up . . .
What is it? The ordinary descriptions never work.

Though surely it has happened to you . . .
When, with one tremendous yawn, you were released
From your body, only to be attacked
By a voice you could not understand.

The voice was within you. It was keeping you
Captive. To be released you had to scream—
But with whose voice? The voice within everyone

So that you are not fully alone? Or a voice
Which rose from within your dream to say
Let us interpret this dream . . .

For even *I* is a dream . . .

4.

A statue may be rising
in the complete nudity
of your own backyard.
It's up to you to decorate it.

Will there be flowers for nipples?
The sky wears the purple of her dress.
Make love to her tonight?
Her name is "Gitanita,"

"Little Gypsy" to the Spaniards.
No one will ever find her, no
no matter how hard they look.

Even the police. Even the man behind me,
about to stab me. Even you, who found her
and lost her the careless day she began to dance.

5.

And somewhere along the line an eye appears
seeing nothing but itself. You are disappointed.
You expected something definite. That the leaves change and fall
just as they're supposed to

is really no answer at all. You want blood,
yes, the future of an emotion
with olives for eyes, with flowers for nipples
and stars like streetlamps giving us directions.

But these ladders never lead anywhere
at all. And like a bundle of heaviness
you once (almost) carried

something always seems to be
flinging itself from your arms
and what is it? This silence that answers

your absence? What commotion, where? Look forward to what?

6.

These ladders never go anywhere
no, and if you step beneath one
you'd better watch out. Clocks warned you. Rain
thwarted you. Dancers and thieves are waiting for you
where? while you are left waiting
where? for something else to take place.

A black cape precedes its entry
into Wall Street at dawn, where
on a clear day, with no memories,
without volition or pangs of regret,
you can see the emptiness rise
like buildings, and the people
dashing in and out, flinging
the emptiness from their outstretched arms.

(1970–1972)

Traces

And then they are there all of the people depressed
Into tattoos or footprints or names plastered
Or carved into wood or wall
Smashing their way through thickets
Or breaking before the seat of a car,
Behind the wave of a smile,
Which is the wave of civilization
Or the crazy past they left behind,
Laughing, as if they are tracing the rotting
Roller-coaster wood into those landsmen's
Plains, the old plains of America's darkness.

(1967)

The Presidential Years

1. In the sixth grade
       Eisenhower to go down to South America
       And Mrs. Goldman to write on the board,
           "Watch C.B.S. Reports tonight on Ike's trip
           And write a report."
       And she to call him "Ike."

   The first summer we went to the country
       And I heard the names Eisenhower and Stevenson,
       And standing there next to the old green Chevrolet
           Looking for a summer bungalow
           Seeing the signs
           And the names Eisenhower and Stevenson
       And asking my mother which is better
       And she says "Stevenson."

   And then on Election Night in 1956
       My sister and I share a room
       And we go to sleep early
       And we do not know who wins until the next morning
   And my mother wakes us up for school
       And my sister asks who won
       And my mother smiles and no, she says, no, we lost.

2. My sisters my cousin Johnny and I sit in the front seats
       Of the car going to my Uncle Bert's
       And my father is driving nervously intently

And Johnny is talking for Israel.
Johnny had a love for Israel unlike anything else.
    He said he wanted to live there.
    He went to college and wrote a good report on Israel
        On all of Israel
        On life in Israel
    And he said when Israel got independence
        There were men real men
        Big husky men who fought for her.
    He said it was terrible what Eisenhower was doing.

I want to know more about "Eisenhower"
    And I get excited and I say Johnny Johnny Johnny
    On his shoulder and I ask him
    And I ask him and he finally says,
"I only said that Stevenson might have been better for Israel."

In Rockaway Beach on a Sunday that summer
The summer of 1957 my father and I went to the beach
    And my father had the *Times*
    And another man asked to see a section
    And pretty soon they had quite a conversation going.
It was Suez U.S. business and Eisenhower and shaking their heads
    And I remember my father saying
    "Don't forget Dulles. It's partly his fault too."
    My father kept repeating that.

And when we came back we went to the synagogue
    And every Saturday my rabbi made a prayer in synagogue
    In English for the government
    And he asked God to protect the president
    And he mentioned the president by name.

And in those years he called out
    "The President of the United States Dwight D. Eisenhower"
        In a loud booming loud booming voice.
        I can still hear him today.

3. In 1959 Ike went to South America
And I had the report to write
And the Dodgers beat the White Sox
In the World Series in an upset.
And I coolly watch the television set and smile
And say to myself that this is the first World Series
I am living through. I am now old enough
To understand what is going on and appreciate
And live it for my team, the Dodgers.
And after we won I walked around triumphantly
And I wore a Los Angeles Dodger baseball cap.

That year too John Kennedy decided on the presidency
And he met in a room in a crucial meeting
To capture the presidency with only the best war
Campaign hardened people. And he talked to the men
And he made plans and they all knew that he would be president.

I went to Canada the summer of the convention.
My father wrote postcards about the convention.
People were hoping that Stevenson would make it,
Stevenson was a fine man.
But Kennedy was nominated and he smiled and he was strong
And my father said that Kennedy certainly knew the Bible
In a fine speech quoting from Isaiah in a fine acceptance speech.

4. In the fall campaign Frank Sinatra
Sang the Kennedy song to the tune of "High Hopes"
In the neighborhood campaign headquarters.

And in the school halls my history teacher danced in
And he came in wearing a straw hat
With the name Kennedy all over it. He was a rabbi
And he told us some days about his grandfather
Who invented a certain type of medical test.
I think it was the scratch test.
This day he came in and sat down and asked us who we were for and why.
Everyone had to stand up and explain.

And only two of us were for Nixon. I got up
And said, "I am for Kennedy for many reasons.
First of all he is a Democrat like Roosevelt.
Also he is for civil rights foreign aid Social Security
And youth. And he will make Adlai Stevenson Secretary
Of State or something, and Chester Bowles too."

The week before the election my rabbi in synagogue
Spoke in the sermon about a man with experience.
I looked at my watch. It had only been five years before
That my rabbi made a sermon that I shall never forget
About a man who fell flat on his face and got up laughing.
He was Eddie Cantor in my mind.

And I had a feeling that Kennedy would win.
On Election Night I told my mother
And she said, "Do you think we're in this time?"

5. In the eighth grade with my red-faced English teacher
In yeshiva. Although it was yeshiva
My English teacher didn't wear a yarmulke. He was not Jewish,
He was Irish. And he breathed hard
Wrote on the board "John F. Kennedy is our President."
And to teach grammar and to illustrate a predicate nominative
        He read the sentence out loud
        And "John F. Kennedy . . . is our President" he says.
I write it down, a neat sentence.

The stock market takes its big tumble.
        My friend Sammy comes over and says
        "We're headed for a depression I know
        My father says we're headed for a depression."
I say we can't have a depression because
There is too little unemployment. We walk down the block.
Sammy is yelling wildly. His father is a member of
The "Save our Business" club. "We're headed for a depression,"
He says. "Look at the stock market. And I don't like it one bit."

I switched to Stuyvesant High School.
    The first day the economics teacher
    Who was very heavy and absentminded and
    Had in his desk 130 typed pages of
    His master's thesis and he picked them up
    And he dropped them on the floor
    Dirty and in jumbled order.

And he asks us about Kennedy slashing the steel prices.
    Larry, a boy with long fingernails
    Who was a Republican was for Rockefeller
    Went home with me every day on the subway,
    Gets up and says, "I am against it.
    Steel companies have the right to raise prices
    Because they haven't done so for years
    And they are entitled to make a profit."
The teacher is reading the thesis he is nodding his head
    Looking up nodding his head frowning nodding
And then he says "no" and mutters about inflation
And says no inflation no that's the right answer
No that's the right answer No.

6. The day that Kennedy was killed
Was the day before the Stuyvesant–Clinton football game.
There was a rally in the auditorium
And our coach who was from Texas or Oklahoma said slowly, carefully,
"There isn't a horse that can't be bucked."

Meanwhile half the school was marching along
    Fifteenth Street to Union Square and then up to
    Forty-second Street and Fifth Avenue and some got up to
    Fifty-ninth, and they were parading,
    Yelling, "De Witt eats shit" until they were stopped by policemen.
        I didn't go. I stayed in school.
        That day I almost got into a fight
        With a fellow twice my size on the stairway
        And he laughed at me. A friend of mine broke it up.

In English the head of the Physics Department walked
Into the room. He said, "I think you are old enough
To understand this. The President was shot today in Texas."
    I stand up. I do not understand. I say, "What"
    And I think, the President was shocked today in Texas.
    He leaves the room. I am sorry.

I leave early. The Clinton game is called off,
    And the series has since been discontinued.
My French teacher is waiting for me. Smiling shuffling his legs
    Touching his teeth with his tongue looking at me
    He says, "There is a rumor that Kennedy was shot.
    Do you know anything about that?"

A week later I go to my cousin's bar mitzvah
        Out in Long Island, and I bring a catalog with me
        From the Bernard Baruch School of City College.
            I want to be a stockbroker.
It is windy outside and we walk a mile or more
        To get to the bar mitzvah
And as I walk I talk to my mother
And I think carefully of what I am to say
And I narrow my eyes.
It is a cold and windy three days after Thanksgiving
And I point my thumb to my stomach and chest
And I brush my scarf against my face
And I say, "I too want to become President."

7. And now I am walking
    After a date with a girl whom I like very much
    And it is a cold February night
    And I am cold
    And the icicles on the cars are like teeth
    And my stuffed nose and ears.
    This is a small city. I can walk across
    This city in an hour. I trot for the last blocks
    Across the bridge.

I am thinking out "The Eisenhower Years" and
"The Kennedy Years" and I am comparing
All the suits the ties the cuff links
The clothes the portraits the graves of all the presidents.
I am passing by all the landmarks the famous landmarks
The places history was made
And I laugh and nod my head and shake my head
And I lower my head and smack my lips
And brace myself for the return home.

And I joke with my girlfriend and my friends
And we walk to the river
And watch the ice melt
And I say, "I too will wind up under the ground."
And they say do not say that.
But I am serious, defiant.
I look at the ice in the river and say,
"We are all going to wind up under the ground."

New York City
March 1967

Notes

"Three 'Dialogues of One'": The title borrows a phrase from the last stanza of John Donne's poem "The Ecstasy."

"Autumn Evening": Unlike the poems "after" Apollinaire, Mayakovsky, and Michaux, "Autumn Evening" is less a translation (or adaptation) than an attempt to simulate a fragment by the German Romantic poet Friedrich Hölderlin.

"In the Queen's Chambers": The Belgian-born Henri Michaux (1899–1984), one of the masters of the French prose poem, invented a stoic and "tractable" character named Plume, to whom misfortunes regularly happen, in *Un certain Plume* (1930). There are thirteen prose poems in the Plume sequence, which Michaux completed in 1936.

"Zone," the central poem in Guillaume Apollinaire's career, prefaces his collection *Alcools*, the title of which translates literally as "Spirits" in the alcoholic sense though I would argue for "Cocktails." *Alcools* is in any case an apt title for one who likes to boast that he has "drunk the universe" and chanted "songs of universal drunkenness." Published in 1913, the year Stravinsky's *Rite of Spring* had its Paris premiere, "Zone" is chronologically the last poem in *Alcools* to have been written. The poet was thirty-three years old, the age of Dante embarking on his tour of the afterlife. The poem doesn't so much praise its objects of futurist desire—the Eiffel Tower, airplanes, a railway terminal—as treat them like pastoral motifs. The heart of the poem is not in the future at all but in a past recollected in anxiety and sadness as the poet walks the streets of Paris. The poem's title embraces (or blends) the meanings of neighborhood, frontier, slum (and slumming), and the female erogenous zone, all of which come into play. ("And I smoke ZONE tobacco," Apollinaire wrote in a later poem.) The celebrated last line, "*soleil cou coupé*," contains a brilliant piece of wordplay that resists the translator's craft. It's as if *cou* (meaning "neck") is an abbreviated form of *coupé* (meaning "cut"). The relation between the two words can be said to suggest the action of the sun rising at dawn and appearing as if beheaded by the horizon. The verse has been variously translated as "Decapitated sun—" (William Meredith), "The sun a severed neck" (Roger Shattuck), "Sun corseless head" (Samuel Beckett), "Sun   slit throat" (Anne Hyde Greet), "Sun neck cut" (Charlotte Mandell). Ron Padgett's "Sun cut throat" cleverly divides the word "cutthroat" in two. I opted for "Let the sun beheaded be," mainly because of the repetition of sounds in the last words. I felt that the relation of "be" to "beheaded" approximated the action in "*cou coupé*." [Note excerpted from *The Virginia Quarterly Review*, 2013]

"Goethe's Nightsong": Johann Wolfgang von Goethe wrote two poems entitled *Wandrers Nachtlied*: the first (*Der du von dem Himmel bist*) in 1776, the one offered here (*Über allen Gipfeln*) in 1780. The poems appear in volume one of Goethe's 1815 *Works* under the headings *Wandrers Nachtlied* and *Ein gleiches* ("Another one"). My father, who lived in Germany until he was twenty-three, knew the poem beginning *Über allen Gipfeln* by heart and sometimes recited it in German, an uncanny gleam in his eyes.

"Cento: The True Romantics": A cento consists entirely of lines lifted from other sources, usually poems. This one is a sonnet furnished from the works of Romantic poets writing in English. "December 14" in *The Daily Mirror* is a second instance of the cento form. "Confessions of a Mask" turns a systematic use of echoes and quotations into something of a structural principle.

"Brooklyn Bridge": Vladimir Mayakovsky (1893–1930) visited New York City in 1925 when Calvin Coolidge was president. Mayakovsky's line about the desperate men has them jumping off the bridge to "the Hudson River," a geographical impossibility. The Brooklyn Bridge spans the East River—you'd have to fly to reach the Hudson on a dive. I was almost tempted to keep the error, because it seems in line with the Russian poet's spectacular hyperboles—and his monumental but always charming self-regard.

From *The Evening Sun: A Journal in Poetry*: To write a journal in verse, not for personal pleasure but for public consumption, is to turn a journalistic form—the daily dispatch from the front—into a poetic one.

Writing *The Evening Sun* I sometimes felt as if I were creating a poetry newspaper that my father could read on the subway ride home from the office if my father were still alive and people still depended on the afternoon paper for late scores and early market returns. . . . As I type these words, Jo Stafford is singing "St. Louis Blues," which protests the setting of the sun. If a melancholic note creeps into these pages it's because I, too, hate to see that evening sun go down. [Note excerpted from *The Evening Sun*, 2002]

From *The Daily Mirror: A Journal in Poetry*: In January 1996 I started writing a poem a day as an experiment. The initial results were not promising. But I kept at it. Toward the end of February I began a consecutive day streak that reached 140. Writing a poem began to seem as natural as taking a walk. There were days I wrote a sestina or a villanelle in addition to the official poem of the day. Poetry was, as one of the poems reported, a renewable energy source. . . . *The Daily Mirror* was the name of a New York morning tabloid that went under as a result of the calamitous newspaper strike of 1962. I liked the idea of a title that would call to mind not only an enchanted glass to be consulted daily, as by a princess in a fairy tale, but also a newspaper to be read by an impatient straphanger on the IRT. . . . The dailiness of the poems may act as a corrective to artificial poetic diction. It may keep the poem honest by rubbing its nose in the details of daily life. . . . The practice of writing a poem a day for any stretch of time obliges the poet, inveterate daydreamer that he is, to be more attentive to his immediate surroundings—the music on the radio, the snow on the ground in the glitter of the sun—than he might otherwise be. [Note excerpted from *The Daily Mirror*, 2000]

"Operation Memory": I've long been fascinated by military code names, such as Operation Torch for the Allied invasion of North Africa in World War II. "Operation Memory" suggested a military metaphor for an autobiographical reflection. Or was memory (or its loss) a metaphor for a military experience? Perhaps both. I set out to write a poem about the war in Vietnam. (An undeclared war, Vietnam is nowhere mentioned in the poem.) "Operation Memory" is a sestina with a variable. Ordinarily, there are six repeating end-words in a sestina. Here there are five fixed end-words and a sequence of numbers where the sixth would go. It's a downward progression (hundred, fifty, eighteen, ten, one) plus a year (1970) and an age (thirty-eight, the age I was when

I wrote the poem). I thought of Abraham trying to persuade God to spare the sinful cities: if there were fifty righteous men, would he do it? If there were twenty righteous men? Ten? I was recently asked whether the speaker commits suicide at the end of the poem ("a loaded gun on my lap"). That's one possibility; a second is that he is about to shoot somebody else; a third is that it's "a loaded gun" in metaphor only. [Note from *The Best American Poetry 1988*]

"Shake the Superflux!" takes its title from King Lear's speech on the heath (act III, scene 4):

> Poor naked wretches, whereso'er you are,
> That bide the pelting of this pitiless storm,
> How shall your houseless heads and unfed sides,
> Your looped and windowed raggedness, defend you
> From seasons such as these? Oh, I have ta'en
> Too little care of this! Take physic, pomp.
> Expose thyself to feel what wretches feel,
> That thou mayst shake the superflux to them
> And show the heavens more just.

As Lear intended it, "superflux" means "surplus" or "superabundance." According to the *OED*, eighteenth-century speakers used the word in the additional sense of "an overflowing, or excessive flow, of water." "Another very remarkable waterfall is the superflux of a collection of water on the top of the high mountain of Mongerlogh," wrote one S. Derrick in 1767. A slightly later entry speaks of "the astonishing supply of water . . . the superflux of which clears all the drains and sewers." [Note from *An Alternative to Speech*, 1986]

Acknowledgments

Amy Gerstler, Roger Gilbert, Glen Hartley, Stacey Harwood, Ron Horning, Lawrence Joseph, and Stephanie Paterik read versions of this manuscript and made valuable suggestions. For advice and support, I would also like to thank Mark Bibbins, Jim Cummins, Denise Duhamel, Alexis Gargagliano, Dana Gioia, Matthew Yeager, David Stanford Burr (who copyedited the manuscript), and the editorial team at Scribner.

The new and previously uncollected poems in this volume appeared originally, sometimes in slightly different form, in various publications, including *The American Poetry Review*, *The American Scholar*, *The Atlantic*, *The Awl*, *Barrow Street*, *Bat City Review*, *Boston Review*, *Columbia Review*, *The Common*, *Conduit*, *Green Mountains Review*, *Hanging Loose*, *The New Criterion*, *The New Republic*, *The New Yorker*, *The Paris Review*, *Partisan Review*, *Poetry*, *Poetry London*, *Slate*, *The Southampton Review*, *The Virginia Quarterly Review*, and as a feature on the website of the Academy of American Poets.

New Poems

The Academy of American Poets ("Poem a Day"): "Autumn Evening"
The American Poetry Review: "1977"
The American Scholar: "Why I Love 'You'"
The Atlantic: "Any Place I Hang My Hat," "The Ides of March"
The Awl: "On the Beautiful and Sublime"
Barrow Street: "The Laffer Curve," "Three 'Dialogues of One'"
Bat City Review: "Lost Weekend"
Boston Review: "Reality Check"

303

The Common: "Mother Died Today"
Conduit: "In the Queen's Chambers"
Green Mountains Review: "Talking to the Present," "Yours the Moon,"
    "The Great Psychiatrist"
Hanging Loose: "The Count"
Hot Street: "Sixteen Tons"
The New Criterion: "The Formula"
The New Republic: "Goethe's Nightsong"
The New Yorker: "Cento: The True Romantics," "The Models"
Poetry: "The Breeders' Cup"
Poetry London: "Ghost Story," "On the Beautiful and Sublime"
Slate: "The Escape Artist"
The Southampton Review: "Sermon on the Mount"
The Virginia Quarterly Review: "Story of My Life," "Zone"

Early and Uncollected Poems

"The Presidential Years": *The Paris Review* #43 (Summer 1968)
"Traces": *The Paris Review* #42 (Spring 1968)
"Goodbye Instructions": *Poetry* (May 1971 and January 1972)
"Simplicity": *Columbia Review* (1972)
"Robert Desnos" in *Some Nerve* (Columbia Review Press, 1973)
"October Classic": *Poetry* (July 1975)
"Nirvana" in *Day One* (Nobodaddy Press, 1979)
"Literal Lives": *The New Republic* (1989)

About the Author

David Lehman is the author of seven previous full-length books of poems: *Yeshiva Boys* (2009), *When a Woman Loves a Man* (2005), *The Evening Sun* (2002), *The Daily Mirror* (2000), and *Valentine Place* (1996), all from Scribner, as well as *Operation Memory* (1990) and *An Alternative to Speech* (1986), both from Princeton University Press. He is the editor of *The Oxford Book of American Poetry* (Oxford University Press, 2006) and series editor of *The Best American Poetry* (Scribner), which he initiated in 1988. In 2010 he won ASCAP's Deems Taylor Award for his nonfiction book *A Fine Romance: Jewish Songwriters, American Songs* (Schocken, 2009). He also wrote and designed the traveling exhibition of the same name, which visited fifty-five libraries in twenty-seven states in 2011 and 2012. Among his other books are a study in detective novels (*The Perfect Murder*, 1989), a group portrait of the New York School of poets (*The Last Avant-Garde*, 1999), and an account of the scandal sparked by the revelation that a Yale University eminence had written for a collaborationist newspaper in his native Belgium in World War II (*Signs of the Times: Deconstruction and the Fall of Paul de Man*, 1991). Lehman has won awards from the Guggenheim Foundation and the American Academy of Arts and Letters. He teaches in the graduate writing program at The New School and lives in New York City and Ithaca, New York.